Family Faith Stories

Books by Ann Weems
Published by The Westminster Press

Family Faith Stories

Reaching for Rainbows:
  Resources for Creative Worship

Family
Faith Stories

Ann Weems

The Westminster Press
Philadelphia

Scripture quotations from the Revised Standard Version of the Bible are copyrighted 1946, 1952, © 1971, 1973 by the Division of Christian Education of the National Council of the Churches of Christ in the U.S.A. and are used by permission.

Book design by Gene Harris

First edition

Published by The Westminster Press®
Philadelphia, Pennsylvania

PRINTED IN THE UNITED STATES OF AMERICA

9 8 7 6 5 4 3 2 1

Library of Congress Cataloging in Publication Data

Weems, Ann, 1934–
   Family faith stories.

   1. Family—Religious life. 2. Barr family.
I. Title.
BV4526.2.W44 1985   248.4   85-13771
ISBN 0-664-24670-2 (pbk.)

To my father,
Thomas Calhoun Barr,
whose life
is a faith story

Contents

Introduction

Whenever there is any sort of family reunion, whether two or ten or more, it takes no time at all for one of us to say, "Do you remember when . . . ?" And everybody nods yes. We all remember, but the storyteller goes right ahead and tells the well-known story anyway, and the others who have heard it a number of times over a number of years go right ahead and laugh or show surprise or horror or whatever emotion the story calls for, just as though they were hearing it for the first time.

During the time we're together, story after story is told, each as exciting and fresh as though it had never been told before. This is the ritual of telling family stories, and everybody loves them because everybody belongs. Everybody knows your name because everybody has the same name, and even if you've never even seen your second cousin twice removed, you're both accepted and loved because you belong to the family.

Family stories. Everybody has them. Everybody loves them. We even love the family stories of other families, and if we tell them to each other long enough, we find how similar our families are—how similar we all are—and we find ourselves belonging to each other, extended family in the family of this earth.

Whenever my parents visited us, my father could hardly get through the door before my children were saying to him, "Tell us about the time when you were a little boy and you went to the movies and you didn't do your homework and you went to school the next day." My father would reply, "You don't want to hear that one again." "Yes, we do!" "Well, maybe after a little while." "Now, please, puh-leese!" Then, with little hands pulling him, he'd go into the living room and sit on the sofa and begin their favorite family story.

My father can sit and tell story after story, and not only are we all enthralled but he himself is so caught up in the memory that he is laughing with the tears running down his cheeks. There's one story he simply cannot finish for laughing so hard. But it's okay; we all know the ending!

Snow and Fire

Winter comes early this year, announcing itself with a rhythmic and unfamiliar *plink-plink* from the living room. I follow the sound, but stop at the window when I see the snow falling, big, fat flakes, one swift upon another on this gray November morning.

The plinking sound comes from the fireplace; the flue has been left open and snow rains upon grate and brick. I close the flue and turn back to the window, drawn magnetically to the falling snow.

I am surprised how quickly the earth is transformed: unraked leaves hidden, tree branches brushed, sidewalk painted, the whole world whitened before my eyes in a matter of minutes. God the artist, painting in white.

Children laugh out of their houses, buttoned into heavy coats and zipped into shiny boots as yet untried. Hats and mittens and an occasional scarf have been found and are in place against the wind and the cold.

Cars are sliding now. The whirring of wheels occasionally mingles with the children's laughter. The students from the university, unprepared for the weather change, rush back from classes for their snow gear. Along the way they pelt each other with snowballs and shout and shove each other into the snow and then duck into their apartment buildings, only to emerge later with a rainbow of winter clothing. A red spaniel runs wildly through the yards, invigorated by the cold of the white stuff, her owner trying unsuccessfully to call her back to the sidewalk.

The first snow! As usual I'm fascinated by it, spellbound by its silent power. What does it mean, this quiet blanketing? What are you telling us, God?

When the snow falls, I want to sit by a fire. I turn again to the fireplace, and inevitably I think of Todd.

Todd always made the fires. That feeling in my chest again. . . . It's been two and a half years and I cannot rid myself of that pain, heavy upon my chest.

The snow comes blurred now. My breathing grows deeper and I ask God, Who's going to make the fire?

I know the answer: Not Todd.

Out loud I cry, "Who's going to make the fires now, God? Tell me that, I AM! Who's going to make the fires now?"

And my tears flow with the falling snow.

Two by two I carry the logs up the stairs—the smaller logs, that is; after repeated back surgery I've learned my limit. Then the kindling, stacked and placed across each other like spokes in a wheel. I reopen the flue. Stuff newspapers under the logs, light them. Watch the fire blaze. Listen to the crackling of the seasoned wood.

I imagine Todd's voice: "That was good, Mom." I smile. "Of course, we could have used a couple of big logs, but under the circumstances, not bad. I knew you could do it."

I sit in front of the fire and look into its flames. Memories dance in fire flames.

Todd's laughing as he brings up the logs. "Now you really want to see the perfect fire? Check it out! I take these logs, see? Big ones. I usually let them season at least six months, but last year's logs are best."

Don grabs him around the waist. "Listen, you little twerp"—Todd's six feet four inches tower over him—"don't lecture me! I was making fires when you were in diapers!"

Todd laughs. "Give it up, Dad!"

Stuart says he'd always built the fires until he went away to school. David says he would build the fires, but Todd always rushes to do it. Todd laughs. "Mom asks me to do it because she wants it done right." The other boys grab him. I think, How like little boys they are! and I remember another Christmas when the three of them, dressed in a variety of red-and-white Christmas pajamas, were caught by the camera in a happy contorted tussle on the same living room floor.

Todd's voice is loud now. "Check it out, Mom! What'd I tell you? It's a work of art!"

I turn and look, and the fire is blazing. "Just like in the movies," he says.

He does know how to lay a fire, that Todd. Todd, the firemaker. "I tell you what," he says, "you can all be my assistants next time. You can bring the logs up!"

"Not me," Heather says. "I'm too little."

Todd blows her a kiss. "I'll bring yours, Miss Pooh," he says. "You know your Todd will always help you."

Todd, laughing . . .

The memory hurts. I look back out at the snow, still falling. The cemetery is beautiful, the black marble stone contrasting with the white of the snow. The stone reads:

WEEMS
TODD CALHOUN

We left Todd there. Oh, Todd, my son, my son. . . .

God is somewhere in the snowing . . .
Unpredictably interrupting the world
    from its drivenness
        if only for a while.
Stop . . . wonder . . . ponder . . .
    and see something beyond
        your own schedules.
Stop . . . and listen to silence,
        snow falling on snow.
I hear a voice asking:
    Who are you?
I search to find an answer;
    I falter: "I am . . . "
And then I see.
I have the eyes to see.
I have the ears to hear.
I see through the falling snow,
I hear through the silence,
I know: I am she who belongs to I AM.

Who Are
Your People?

Memories dance in the flames of fires. Other fires . . . other
times . . . other boys . . . my brothers, bringing wood in for
the fires. We lived in an enormous manse that had four
fireplaces: one in the living room, one in Daddy's study, two
in the bedrooms upstairs. It was Christmas and my mother
wanted a fire. We couldn't put up the Christmas tree until
after Sunday because we held the worship service in this
living room. It was a young church, and worship services
would be held there until we could afford to build. My father
followed the boys in through the door that I held for them.
He was carrying the heaviest logs in his arms and bent
forward so that his sweater was hiked up in the back. He
directed the laying of the fire, but my brother Tommy
added plenty of comments. My mother kept throwing
scraps of paper in the fireplace with no reverence for the
ritual.

Tommy decided he wanted to light the fire by rubbing
two sticks together. We all kept an eye on my younger
brother, Bill, who had already set a field aflame. Finally it
was time for the Opening of the Flue, a family tradition
handed down for generations and still practiced in our
home today: Is the flue open? Or is it closed? How do you
know? Are you sure? Pull it up; pull it down. Then we have
the speech of reassurance by that person who has been

chosen for this role in the family. "The flue is up; it's open. When you lay a fire, push up. That opens the flue."

Everyone was convinced . . . sort of. Matches appeared. We couldn't wait for two sticks to spark. My brother was disgusted with our impatience. He mumbled something about what if we were lost in the woods and we wanted to start a fire so that we could be rescued. We all stared at him. We lighted the fire. My sister, Jane, and I sat by the fire playing paper dolls until we were called to bed.

God, you who speak through falling snow, do you speak through fire flames? What do you want me to see? What do you want me to hear?

I get up and move back to the window. A father has gone to pick up his child at the nursery school at the Methodist church. His voice comes clear and deep through the snow, through the window, through the silence. "Did you see what happened while you were in school? It snowed! I brought the sled to bring you home."

Home. Where was he from? I know a southern accent when I hear one! It reminded me of the time when I was in Madison, Wisconsin, leading the worship at an Interim Ministers' Conference, and before supper that first night a man with a pronounced southern accent came up to me and asked, "Where are you from?"

"Tennessee," I answered. "Nashville."

He smiled. "I knew it," he said. Then he looked me straight in the eye and asked, "Who are your people?"

Who are your people? A surge of memories swept over me. He had detected my own southern accent. "Who are your people?" In my mind's eye I saw faces and names and even smelled some of the sweet aromas that I associate with home.

"Who are your people?" I knew what he meant. I had answered that question when I went off to college in Memphis. I had answered that question when I married and my name changed. I knew what it meant: To whom do you belong? Who is your family? It is an ancient question. Who

18

is your clan? Who is your tribe? It's a means of identification, a claiming of ties. Sometimes it means acceptance; sometimes it means rejection. By the world's standards it can separate the somebodies from the nobodies. Sometimes it instantly opens doors; sometimes it closes them.

I knew what he meant, and yet what sprang to my mind as an answer was: My father was a wandering Aramean. Deuteronomy 26:5–11:

> "A wandering Aramean was my father; and he went down into Egypt and sojourned there, few in number; and there he became a nation, great, mighty, and populous. And the Egyptians treated us harshly, and afflicted us, and laid upon us hard bondage. Then we cried to the LORD the God of our fathers, and the LORD heard our voice, and saw our affliction, our toil, and our oppression; and the LORD brought us out of Egypt with a mighty hand and an outstretched arm, with great terror, with signs and wonders; and he brought us into this place and gave us this land, a land flowing with milk and honey. And behold, now I bring the first of the fruit of the ground, which thou, O LORD, hast given me." And you shall set it down before the LORD your God, and worship before the LORD your God; and you shall rejoice in all the good which the LORD your God has given to you and to your house, you, and the Levite, and the sojourner who is among you.

My father was a wandering Aramean. It came to mind because I know to whom I belong. That, however, as an answer to this man would have been misunderstood. I knew what he meant. I was a Southerner and I knew what he meant. *Who are your people?*

"My father is Tom Barr," I answered.

A look of surprise and recognition and delight came over the man's face. He turned around to a number of people with him and said, "She's one of us! She's Tom Barr's daughter."

Instant acceptance! They gathered around me and led me to their table, where we talked about all the people I had known twenty-five years ago when I lived in Nashville. It was an incredible dash back into time and it felt good. Warm.

19

It felt right. I belonged. I was accepted. I was Tom Barr's daughter. And Tom Barr is a Presbyterian minister and the people we talked about were mostly Presbyterians or Nash-villians or South Carolinians, since that's where our people are from, South Carolina.

Can you imagine? Everybody knows your name! I was reminded of the Broadway musical in which a young girl sings much the same thing.

I know who my people are. They are the children of a wandering Aramean.

Our faith story begins with an ending:
　　the ending of slavery in Egypt.
In the beginning was the Word
　　and the Word was with God
　　and the Word was God.
And the Word of God
　　has always had to do
　　with the ending of slavery.
In the beginning was the Word
　　and the Word was with God
　　and the Word was Creation.
In the beginning was the Word
　　and the Word was with God
　　and the Word became flesh
　　and dwelt among us.
We in the church
　　must be about our business
　　of ending slavery
　　and beginning anew,
For Christ is the New Creation.

A Wandering Scot

Our father was for sure a wandering Scot, one of those Scottish Dissenters who sought religious freedom. Neither the Aramean nor the Scot would live in slavery. Both sought to worship God in freedom. Some of the Scottish Calvinists migrated to Ireland, where they found their lot no better than it had been in Scotland. They gladly sailed for Carolina, where they felt it was better to face a wilderness than to have to conform to worship dictated by others.

Family historians can definitely trace the Barrs back to James, but since they have found the will of a William Barr who had a son named James who was in the same region in Williamsburg County, the assumption is that William was the father of James. Furthermore, a George Barr is named as one of the founders of the Presbyterian Church in Indiantown, South Carolina, in 1757. He's listed as one of the first county settlers in Boddie's *History of Williamsburg County, S.C.* There was also a Margaret Barr Drew who died in 1762 and a Sarah Barr Montgomery who died in 1770. Since William Barr died in 1764, the assumption is that George, William, Margaret, and Sarah were brothers and sisters. There's also talk in the family that their father was Chalmers and that he came with them from Scotland. Whether they were in Ireland or not, we're not sure. My own children, with the exception of Stuart, who's always been interested in history of any kind, say, "Who cares?" I care. When I sing "Faith of Our Fathers," I'm singing about Abraham, Isaac, and Jacob, but I'm also singing about George and James and William—even Chalmers!

A wandering Scot was my father, and he decided to leave Scotland so that he might worship according to his conscience. His first priority was religious freedom, and so when he made his way to Carolina he settled on the lower reaches of the Black River in that part of Craven County later known as Williamsburg, and he joined in public worship at the king's tree. We call this branch of the family the Kingstree Barrs.

Chalmers, if indeed the Barrs can claim him as our Scot, was one of these. William was certainly one of these. He settled in Craven County some years before the Revolution. He was a very devout man and set about providing for his family and his faith in the wilderness of Carolina. Although there is no record of his first land grant, he did very well for an individual in prerevolutionary days. At the time of his death, his plantation was worth £480, or $2,400. In addition he owned 19 head of cattle, 14 horses, 8 hogs, and many bushels of rice, barley, oats, flaxseed, potatoes, and corn. He owned a plow, 3 guns, 1 crosscut saw, a parcel of plantation tools ("and other tools too tedious to mention"). My mother was sorry to hear he listed no silver, but he did list pewter and a looking glass, 2 chests, and 5 beds and a child's cradle. This inventory was valued at £1,256. William did very well for himself in this wilderness.

Did my wandering Scot compare himself and the people who crossed the sea with him with the children of Israel going into the wilderness? How strong a faith my fathers and mothers had! They were not willing to serve other gods. They didn't rationalize that they were better off staying in a situation that did not allow them to worship as their consciences saw fit. They lived in faith and they lived in hope.

Carolina held hope for these Scots, hope that their searching would cease. What was it my father William (or even Chalmers) saw, looking around this new land? He found a land rich in planting soil, abundant with game, and offering a variety of trees: hickory, oak, ash, poplar, sweet gum, and black gum as well as pine.

Of course, the Scots also had to face quite a few hardships. Clearing the land was difficult. The very conditions that yielded plentiful crops also made for a thick wilderness. Wild animals were a daily threat: wolves and bears and panthers. The hot South Carolina sun must have been a challenge to people who were used to living in the colder climates of Ireland and Scotland. Then there was always the fear of disease, although the Scots were a hardy lot and seemed to withstand plenty.

I wonder if William wasn't one of those who succumbed to the fever. Family historians date his birth about 1710 and do know for sure that he made a will in July of 1764 and died in November, age fifty-four. What happened in July to prompt him to make a will?

A will is a mine of information. No church records have remained from that day, no birth certificate is available for William, no Bible has been passed down with carefully written dates in it, but from William's will we learn quite a lot. He was certainly a man of faith. He asks God's forgiveness for any sins, "being penitent and sorry from the bottom of my heart." He asks that his worldly possessions be divided between his wife and his eleven children, except "for the Book." It was the custom for devout men to leave their Bible to their favorite child. There is no record of who got the Bible.

This strikes me as a custom that is unkind. To name a most-loved child would certainly hurt the other children. It also strikes me as very biblical: Abraham and Isaac, Isaac and Esau, Rebecca and Jacob, Jacob and Joseph—the list goes on—David and Absalom . . . very biblical.

William had eleven children and nine of them had biblical names: James, Isaac, Nathan, Rachel, Caleb, Jacob, Silas, Esther, and John. The oldest, a daughter, was named Margaret, probably after William's sister, perhaps after William's mother, too. The youngest one William named after himself.

William was probably married twice because the older children, the first three, are named first and left an English shilling apiece, showing he had already given them their portion. Then his wife, Esther, and the remaining eight children are named.

Oh, William, I sit here in front of the fire and the falling snow and I wonder about the wilderness that all of us have to face. You were a child of God who cared so much about your faith that you crossed an ocean for it, cleared a wilderness for it, named your children after those children of God in another land and another time. And you held your Book dear to you. Did your father give it to you? Or your mother on a cold day in Scotland?

I have Todd's Book and my mother Gladys's Book, and I take them out and hold them and read what they wrote in the margins and reread what is underlined and treasure them. I wonder if your Book is still in existence. Does some descendant have it and is it on a coffee table or in an attic or is it read and treasured?

Who are your people? My people are those who read the Book and listen beside a fire or in a wilderness for the still small voice of I AM. My father is he who worships even if it is beneath the king's tree. My father is he who builds a church when he comes into the wilderness. My father is he who cherishes his Book.

God heard the groaning of the Scots
    and led them out of the land of Scotland
    to the shores of South Carolina.
And there,
    remembering their father Noah,
they first knelt beneath the king's tree
    and worshiped God,
      who had heard their crying
        and had led them to this promised land.
They built,
    they educated,
      they worked.
But first they knelt.
First, they were God's.
God-directed, they sought this land first of all
    to worship
        freely.

Faith

What I'm wondering as I sit cozy by the fire and watch the snow still falling in the St. Louis sky is, What did you Scots suffer during the Revolution, father James? Plantations were burned, cattle and sheep were destroyed, crops were ruined. Did you live in fear every day? Did your boys go to war? Did Sarah, your wife, weep because she had no word? The whole district lived in the midst of war; a daily dirge was sung for those who fell. A daily fear was your lot, for you never knew when it would be your plantation, your wife and children, you. . . .

Then one night a particularly cruel and unwarranted act: The Indiantown Church was burned to the ground. Nothing saved. What you had built to the glory of God went up in smoke, burned because "it was a sedition shop."

Irony of ironies. . . . It was Major James Wemyss, another Scot, loyal to the crown, who "laid waste a tract of country between Black River and the Pee Dee seventy miles in length and in some places fifteen miles wide" (Wallace, South Carolina). "On most of the plantations every house was burned to the ground, the negroes were carried off, the inhabitants plundered, the stock, especially the sheep, wantonly killed; and all provisions, which could be come at, destroyed." It was this Major Wemyss who burned the church of my fathers and mothers at Indiantown. The irony is that James Wemyss was one of the immigrant ancestors

27

of the American Weems family. Both he and James Barr are the fathers of my children!

With the church burned, all records were burned too. In wartime people are not apt to stop and try to reassemble records and then it is forgotten, but the Barrs know that the people of the Indiantown Church worshiped in a nearby field or under a bush arbor, for George Barr, one of the sons of James, was baptized out of doors in 1781.

Who are my people? My people are those who worship through the fighting and baptize their children even if there is no building. I can visualize James and Sarah and their little George standing in the Carolina sun, asking that their child be blessed, be received by their God who was their God through persecution and war. In the flames of my fire I see the flames of the fire of the Indiantown Church and I see the Scots, my fathers and mothers, praying for peace, praying for the strength to rebuild their homes and their church, praying that the children being baptized might be enabled to live and worship in a world without religious and civil persecution.

Ours is the faith
    that directs our coming in and our going out,
the faith
    that orders our lives,
the faith
    that demands risk and standing up and speaking
        out,
the faith
    that asks us to believe and to love,
the faith
    that asks us to live all the rest of our days
        for the furthering of the Kingdom of God.

Serious and Strict

The Barrs have always been great tellers of tales, and whenever a few of us are gathered together, you can be sure there will be a lot of laughter. In fact, some stories cannot be finished because the storyteller is actually dissolved in tears from laughing so hard. I've heard great-aunts and great-grandmothers giggling like schoolgirls, and a few years back my father and his brother, Walter, were telling stories about their grandfather, and neither of them could say more than a word at a time without being overcome with laughter, eyes filled and ribs hurting.

However, there was a very serious and strict Barr who was an elder in the Indiantown Church at a time when he and the rest of the elders saw fit to discipline other members of the church. George Barr, son of James, was elected elder in 1819. The church had already set down some rules to try to curb intemperance.

1. Private drunkenness to be admonished.
2. Drunkenness not "aggravated by profanity, contention, or some other immorality" to be reproved by the Session.
3. Aggravated drunkenness to be reproved before the congregation.
4. Persistence in intemperance to be punished by being cut off from the communion of the church.

If the offender did not change his ways quickly, he was suspended; and if he continued to offend, he was excommunicated.

In 1818 the higher authorities of the General Assembly denounced dancing. The congregation had always enjoyed dancing and horse racing and moderate drinking. The Session did not really act until the arrival of the Rev. John McKee Erwin in December of 1828.

On January 8, 1830, the Session unanimously resolved to address the following to the Communing Members of this society:

> That whereas your Session has reason to believe that some of the members in full communion in the Church give encouragement to and take an active part in Balls or Dancing frolics, and whereas the encouragement thus given to this amusement is a great grievance to Some, perhaps to a Majority of this Society, and, if we mistake not, a Stumbling Block to others; and whereas the General Assembly of our Church has expressly disapproved of this Amusement as inexpedient among professors in our Church; the Session after deliberately viewing these things in connection with our high responsibilities as officers of this Church do hereby declare to you our approval of the decision of this Judicatory of our Church and that we will henceforth feel ourselves bound to view all professors of religion in this Church who encourage or take an active part in dancing as offenders against Its purity and prosperity; and finally Brethren we affectionately exhort you to abstain from all appearance of evil, directed to be read by the Moderator next Sabbath.

Evidently the direction was not altogether adhered to, because on March 27 the minister was instructed to "admonish privately" those who offended. Still the dancing continued. So the Session asked Presbytery, "What further measures if any are to be taken?" Presbytery answered that the Session was to adhere "to the Book of Discipline and the expressions of the opinion of the Synod and General Assembly" (March of 1831).

The Session sent some of the elders to admonish the

dancers, "to bring them to Repentance." One of the members who continued to have dancing parties was Sam McGill, who was the grandson of one of the founders of the church. Mr. McGill quoted from Isaac Watts: "Religion never was designed to make our pleasures less."

Dr. Samuel Davis McGill, son of the offender, later wrote in *Reminiscences in Williamsburg County:*

> The Rev. J. M. Erwin, from North Carolina . . . tall and slim of figure, and of cold and repulsive address, condemned from the pulpit the practice of dancing. . . . A church committee, composed of the elders of the church, was appointed to wait on Mr. Samuel McGill to summon him to trial to be held in the session house. When the day came those two men were seen approaching his house and as their errand was known, it can be imagined in the manner his soft blue eyes sparkled with indignation, overshadowing his otherwise handsome features. He did not meet them, but the wife did at the gate, and it was said their business was hurriedly dispatched amid her clamors, made stinging by her nimble and then irritated tongue, telling them, among other things, of Mr. McGill's claim to that church which his father had founded, nor did she desist in the denunciation of them till they were out of her hearing, and going at a brisker pace than they had come.

Was one of those chosen for this unhappy errand our George Barr?

Mr. McGill was tried for obstinacy and disrespect of "the authoritative expression of the General Assembly in 1818" and slandering an individual of this Session. He was found guilty of the first two charges and ordered to appear before the elders and witnesses for admonition. He asked that he appeal to the congregation, but Presbytery said that was unconstitutional. Harmony Presbytery discussed the whole matter at its next meeting and upheld the decision of the Session. Later Mr. McGill appeared before the Session and confessed and made his peace and, according to his son, "There were no more dancing parties given at his house during the remainder of his life."

Others were accused and some were suspended while

George Barr served on the Session during this troublesome time. Mr. McGill was a highly respected member of the church and the community, and the decision was an unpopular one.

In 1834, the Session addressed the congregation:

> April 28th. We the undersigned, Elders of the Indiantown Church, having for some years past been contending against prevailing practices in the Church, which we deem unchristian and when bringing discipline to bear on offending members, we were plainly told by a member in full standing "that he knew the mind of the congregation ten times better than we did and that there were not three individuals in Indiantown Church that would sustain our proceedings," and having received very little Support or Countenance from the Congregation, we were induced to believe his statements measurably correct, and moreover at a House in the immediate vicinity of the Church (the Heads of the family in full membership) at which a large number of the Congregation attended a Wedding, on the night previous to a three days' meeting, at which the Sacrament of the Lord's Supper was administered, these practices were introduced and persevered in through the night and to such excess that we believe it hopeless to proceed farther against such determined opposition, and as we cannot Conscientiously Serve the Church as Ruling Elders, seeing the practice of dancing, excessive drinking, and their accompanying evils cannot be Suppressed by us, and judging from the efforts already made that our influence is insufficient for this or to promote the purity and edification of this Church; and therefore after mature reflection we have unanimously resolved that we claim the Constitutional privilege of ceasing to act as officers of this Congregation . . . and now we earnestly pray the Great Head of the Church that the efforts of those who may be called in His Providence to Succeed us may be accompanied with His Almighty power and blessing and make theirs more successful than ours have been.

The Signers: S. James Wilson, George Barr, George McCutcheon, and David D. Wilson.

Poor George Barr and the other elders. They were trying

to fulfill their responsibilities as elders and took that responsibility seriously. In the Session record book at Indiantown, there is a notation that George's brother James was suspended. I don't know if he skipped church too often or if he drank or danced or if he was just plain "contumacious"!

It is on record that some of the dancers were judged contumacious because they did not stop their dancing. "Contumacious" means stubbornly resisting or disobeying authority. I'd forgotten all about the word, but isn't it a wonderful one?! I'd venture to say that many a Barr since Uncle George would be called contumacious. Of course, when it is applied to some of us, we would call our position integrity or conscience. Anyway, Uncle George and the other elders were doing the calling, and "contumacious" was what they called several members of the Indiantown Church. Finally the Session resigned, unable to stand up to the contumacious attitude of the congregation.

Mr. Erwin left shortly thereafter, to go back to North Carolina. The history titled *Indiantown Presbyterian Church, 1757–1957*, collected and arranged by James F. Cooper, explains: "Members of the congregation still danced, and the Session still thundered; but there seems to have been a more perfunctory approach to discipline. Sinners were quick to confess, but almost as quick to fall from grace again." More resolutions and more contumacious attitude on the part of the congregation. In 1861 (the year after George died), William Chalmers Barr and D. D. Barr and D. D. Wilson resigned because they had "lost the confidence of the congregation." History repeats itself!

I expect that George Barr would have had trouble keeping his fun-loving descendants off the dance floor, but he had a reputation as a sincere and upstanding man in both church and community.

When my father and daughter and I walked through the cemetery at the Indiantown Church, we made a rubbing of George's gravestone. It reads:

SACRED
To the Memory of
GEORGE BARR
The deceased was born in the Year 1781
And died 1st August 1860.
In the eightieth year of his age.
He was for many years a consistent
Member of Indiantown Church.
And served as a Ruling Elder of the
Same for a period of Forty Years.

These verses are written below:

> How blest the righteous when he dies,
> When sinks a weary soul to rest,
> How mildly beam the closing eyes,
> How gently heaves the expiring breast.
> Life's duty done as sinks the day,
> Light from its load, the Spirit flies,
> While Heaven and Earth combine to say,
> How blest the righteous when he dies.

Who are my people? They are those who try to live right-eously, but who admit to the anxieties of the responsibility of faith!

Sometimes
 in the stress of life
we feel overwhelmed
 by the responsibility
 of faithfulness.
Sometimes
 we feel
 that we are right,
 and others,
 equally as faithful,
 feel that they are right.
O God, wouldn't it have been easier
 on all of us
 if you had written down the rules?—
 if you had spelled it out?
 NO DANCING
 or
 DANCING OKAY.
This freedom thing
 that you have handed us
 is not easy . . . not easy at all.
Perhaps the question is not about dancing
 (or all the other choices we Christians argue about);
Perhaps the question of faithfulness has to do with
 what is written on our hearts.

Community of Worship

My father told me that his grandfather Barr (George Daniel) used to tell the grandchildren about playing with the Indians when he was growing up. Grandfather Barr was an expert shot with rifle or with bow and arrow. He made his grandsons bows and arrows and would tell them about shooting contests with the Indians. When he won, the Indians would give him a bow and arrow; if they won, he would give them a plug of tobacco.

My great-grandfather used a slate in his early years in school. Later he used paper and lead pencils made of flattened buckshot stuck in canes. I thought the other day how much Great-Grandfather Barr would love this word processor his great-granddaughter owns. He wouldn't have been intimidated by computers; he loved to tinker with things and figure out how to make life easier.

When George was sixteen, he was sent to school in Virginia. However, he never arrived. When the stagecoach stopped in Greenville, South Carolina, he got out to replace a lost hat and started chatting with some men there, and they told him about the Thalian Academy near Pendleton. The school was directed by a Dr. J. L. Kennedy. It sounded good to George. Why go all the way to Virginia? He could be close to the Barr relatives if he stayed in South Carolina.

When George Barr decided to go to the Thalian Academy, he boarded with Major Thomas H. McCann, who lived across the street from the academy.

In the dining room at my brother Bill's home in Tennessee hang portraits of Major and Mrs. McCann. Since George married their oldest daughter, Martha Jane, they were my great-great-grandparents.

My mother used to tell us . . . and tell us . . . and tell us again that we were descended from the Royal House of Stuarts on three sides of the family. We used to tease her about it because she was so diligent in her research and longed for one of us to be interested. We were always interested in the mavericks in the family, which she tried to hush up as soon as she knew we were listening. It was through the McCanns that we attain my mother's dream of being descendants of royalty.

In the 1700s, Patrick McCann of Scotland, who was married to Jane Stuart of the Royal House of Stuart, migrated with her to Northern Ireland. A son, Robert, was born to them in Killileagh, Ardegan, in 1764. Robert and his wife, Jane Hamilton, Thomas McCann's parents, came to America in 1783.

Everybody in the family calls him Major McCann, and from where I sat in Bill's dining room he was a most imposing gentleman. He was a leader in Carmel Presbyterian Church in Pickens County. The Carmel Church was organized in 1789, and when a group organized the First Presbyterian Church of Greenville in 1848, it was Major McCann who offered a resolution to the congregation of Carmel Church, then a strong and wealthy organization, "to take up a collection for the feeble First Presbyterian Church colony of Greenville." Today that Greenville church is strong and vital.

I've never understood those who say
    they don't need the church.
Mine is a profound need
                        to worship
    and to live
        in solidarity with the community of the faithful.
Of course, I can pray by myself
        and make decisions by myself,
            but it has to be in the context of the covenant
            that you and I have with God.
To love mercy in the midst of the unmerciful,
        to do justice in the jaws of injustice,
            to be humbly aware of God's grace
        takes constant communion with God and the
                community.
To me, being faithful assumes Life in this community
        which Christ called his church.
To me, the church is home.

Ah, Greenville!

Ah-h-h-h, Greenville! As a child I loved going to Greenville, where all those laughing Barrs joined together to eat a meal you've never seen the likes of. The thing about being a Barr was that everybody loved you just because you had the right name. It was always a rollicking time because there were so many of us. Daddy was one of eight children and his father was one of six and his mother was one of eight.

I've seen pictures of Greenville in the early days, and Daddy and Heather and I drove around the town with Daddy telling us where it was he lived when he was a little boy. We went to the houses we visited as children, when Aunt Lena lived next door to Dan-Dan (our grandmother), and we went to the spot where Grandpa had his tin shop.

In 1872, George Daniel Barr decided to move his family to Greenville, where he opened a machine shop and hardware store. He was awfully clever at fixing things. So the good people of Greenville brought their problems to my great-grandfather and he solved them. He was also an inventor.

He invented one of the first bottle fillers used in drugstores. He got two thousand dollars for this invention, a very large amount in those days.

My father said his grandfather had all sorts of inventions and was famous for his glue recipe. Annie Barr Anderson copied it from the recipe book of Grimke Rhett, 21 Broad Street, Charleston, South Carolina:

MR. BARR'S RECEIPT FOR GLUE

' oz. gum Arabic	Boil until well dissolved
½ oz. Isinglass	in water enough to make
	thin paste. When needed
	for use, warm.

I wonder if that was ever patented. I wonder if it's good. I wonder if I could find isinglass!

I have a picture of this great-grandfather and great-grandmother surrounded by their family. It was taken in the brick house on the corner of Broad and Main streets. They're sitting in the middle of their six children, the children's spouses, the grandchildren. He looks like a man happy with his life, happy with his family, proud even. He's wearing a mustache and a very long beard that falls from his chin only.

I have another picture of my great-grandfather taken later, in 1902, about ten years after the first picture, and he had shaved off his beard. Although he was a man of sixty-six, he looks much younger. Maybe it was because he never lost the zest for living. There was always another hymn to sing, another expedition to take the boys on, another invention, another something to fix.

In Greenville, George Daniel Barr was an elder in the First Presbyterian Church, where his grandchildren and great-grandchildren are still members. All his sons—my Grandfather Walter, Uncle Louie, and Uncle George T.— were elders in that church. The minister, Dr. T. W. Sloan, was a good friend of my grandfather's and a good friend to my father.

Mr. Arthur G. Gower, in the seventy-fifth anniversary booklet of the church, wrote in 1923:

> The synonym for Barr in relation to this church has been faithfulness. Mr. G. D. Barr, the patriarch of this flock, Wal-

ter, George, and Louis, the sons, were all honored by the Church in selection to office and in turn were an honor to the Church in the fulness of their service. Then, too, the daughters were no whit behind the sons, Misses Bessie and Annie and "Daylight" were and still are faithful and loyal to their Lord in their service.

From 1880 on, one cannot fail to be impressed with the ingathering of the grandchildren of the earlier members of the Church. The beacon lights which long ago may have blazed so brightly, and now have grown dim with age or gone out in death, are reconsecrated in these young people who are so filially and zealously taking their forefathers' place in Church and general Christian effort.

It is remarkable: This son of the son of the son of the son of the Scot who came to these shores seeking a place where he could worship faithfully . . . this son passing his faith on to his sons and daughters, and, of course, the story is multiplied in uncles and aunts and cousins.

These people who lived six generations back
                              and I . . .
We are linked forever throughout history.
I am flesh of their flesh,
                         but even more,
    I am heart of their hearts,
For who they are
                they gave away to those of us
                         who followed . . .
And the children of Israel
    (back generation after generation after generation)
And I
       are linked together throughout eternity,
For in the beginning
                     was the Word
    and through time
       the Word
                 is spoken.
Those who hear the story
                        live
                    abundantly,
       the love of God written on their hearts.

Between the Hurt
and the Heart

And mothers! How many times I have written "father" because that was the news of import of the day, but how often I've wondered about those mothers of mine. I don't have as much information, but I know what it is to be a mother, to be a woman in a world dominated by men. My generation is the link generation, women hitting middle age when the feminist movement has really caught hold, women who are pulled in different directions by demands from self and from home. But my mothers didn't know these rules; theirs was a male-dominated world and they fit in as best they could. From what I've learned about them, they did it well!

The obituary of Martha Jane McCann Barr, my great-grandmother, states:

> Mrs. Barr possessed a Christian character and disposition that was singularly sweet and attractive. She was one of the quiet ones whose sphere is home, and there she ruled with queenly grace. She was devoted to her family, her church, and her God, and this community is enriched by such lives as hers.

When my father suggested that he and Heather and I go to Ninety Six, South Carolina, I couldn't believe there really was such a place, but there in the cemetery next to the old Rock Presbyterian Church lie the Stuarts, my grandmother's people. We went to Ninety Six after my mother died. I thought how she would have reveled in the history of the Stuart clan. Yes, this was the second line of Stuarts. It was almost as though Gladys was saying, "See, I told you that you were descended from the Royal House of Stuarts." I hear you, Mother.

There on the stones were the family names that keep reappearing, even more so than in the Indiantown cemetery. Stuart is our oldest son's name (and there are other Stuarts in the Barr clan). In the front of the cemetery is a large stone with Stuart on it, J. A. Stuart. That's Dr. John Alexander Stuart, my great-grandfather, and I wish I could have known him. I've heard and read nothing but praise about this man. He, like Great-grandfather Barr, was orphaned when he was quite young. He, too, had inheritance enough to get a good education.

Dr. Stuart's closest friend was Col. Larkin Griffin. Larkin Griffin, my great-great grandfather, was born on March 21, 1788, in Laurens County, South Carolina. You will be surprised to hear that he was not a Presbyterian but a Baptist! Not only a Baptist, but a very faithful and ardent one. He was the youngest of seventeen children of Richard and Nancy Clark Griffin, who had moved from Culpepper County, Virginia.

Larkin Griffin was a builder and contractor and very good at his work. He amassed a considerable fortune before the war. But first and foremost in his life was his faith, so much so that when the Baptist Church asked him to oversee the building of the Baptist Seminary in Greenville, he broke up his farm and moved his family to Greenville for the duration of the construction. After the project was completed, the family returned home.

Both Dr. Stuart and Colonel Griffin were community-minded men and became the best of friends. The story is that Dr. Stuart asked for the hand of Colonel Griffin's daughter, Eliza B. Griffin. Colonel Griffin was delighted. Tragically, Eliza died just sixteen months after their marriage.

In the cemetery at the old Rock Presbyterian Church is Eliza's grave. There is a curious mistake on her stone; it reads: Born April 15, 1825, died May 17, 1813. The mistake was never rectified. I suppose the *1* was supposed to be a *4* so that it should read 1843. She would have been eighteen. That was the first of their eleven children that Larkin and Jemima Griffin buried.

Next Dr. Stuart married the second daughter of Colonel Griffin, Tabitha. She, too, died after a short marriage. Then Dr. Stuart asked for the hand of Mary Parthenia Griffin, and Colonel Griffin is reported to have answered, "Well, John, you can have her, but I want you to know that you cannot have the old lady until I'm dead."

An Irishman came to Ninety Six and was not there long before he became seriously ill. He went to my great-grandfather Stuart and asked for help, and Dr. Stuart insisted that he stay with them until he was on his feet again. Aunt Lena says her father cared for people way beyond the call of duty. When the man recuperated, he wanted to do something for them, so, since he was a bricklayer, he built a greenhouse onto the side of the house and it was glorious. Aunt Lena says the fuchsias were incredible and the greenhouse was jammed with flowering plants that could take your breath away.

During the War Between the States, Brother Tom, who was sixteen at the time, took the horses and the silver down by the river and hid them both so that they wouldn't be taken. His father needed the horses for getting to his sick patients. The Union men never knew they were there.

Once when Dr. Stuart was gone, three Union officers rode up with their brigade. They came to the front door and asked Great-grandmother Stuart if they might have some lunch. She said they were very polite. She told them she would be happy to feed them, and she prepared a meal and sat down to lunch with them. The men of the company remained outside. It was spring and my great-grandmother's plum trees were laden with plums, not yet ripe for picking. She had every intention of making damson preserves as soon as they ripened. From the dining room window, she looked and saw the men of the Union Brigade

46

wantonly hitting at those plum trees, knocking the unripe plums to the ground. She looked at the lieutenant and asked if he would please speak to his men about the plum trees. The men were not eating them, as they weren't yet ripe enough, but were just swinging at them, knocking one after another to the ground. The officer excused himself and spoke to the men, and they stopped and he returned to the table. That evening when Dr. Stuart came home, the whole incident was related to him and he looked at his wife and asked, "Weren't you afraid of the Union officers?" His wife answered, no, she had prepared a delicious meal for them and they had behaved themselves like gentlemen, and she didn't feel that they would see any sense in ruining the plum trees. Evidently they didn't!

Uncle Walter and my father remember going into their grandmother's kitchen when she lived in Greenville and being scared by the "leather britches hanging across the room." I asked them what "leather britches" were. They said they were green beans hung to dry, but that in the shadows of that kitchen they looked particularly scary, like long fingers ready to reach out and grab little boys in the dark.

Great-great-grandfather Larkin and Great-great-grandmother Jemima came to live with the Stuarts in Ninety Six after Colonel Griffin retired and Mrs. Griffin broke up housekeeping. It was a happy household, full of good times and care for the family as well as other people in the community.

John's sister was married to Mary's brother, which made them double in-laws. John's sister died, probably of some fever because then, before 1860, John Griffin, who was also a doctor in the Cokesbury district, died, leaving two young boys. Without a moment's hesitation, Mary and John took the boys into their already large family and raised them.

With her great love of shrubs and plants as well as her great love of her church, Mary Stuart decided to give the Rock Presbyterian Church some banana trees. They were put by the side of the church in the adjoining cemetery. Her sisters' graves were there and those of other family and friends. The banana trees did so beautifully that the children of the congregation on their way to Sunday school would help themselves to bananas. This was all right, but finally the elders had to ask Mary to please remove them as the children were trampling over the graves to get to the bananas! She replaced them with something a little less tempting.

When Daddy and Heather and I went to Ninety Six, a woman was lovingly working with the plants and shrubbery. She was a doctor's wife, a lovely woman with an obvious green thumb, who was giving her talents away for the church she, too, loved. That was you, Mary Stuart, giving your considerable talent and care and comfort to your dear husband, to the family, to the church, and to the community. I am glad to call you mother!

When you planted those banana trees you had no idea what would happen that summer of 1876. Typhoid fever settled its deadly cloud over the little community of Ninety Six, and Dr. Stuart, who gave comfort and healing to so many, was away from home most of the time, nursing the sick. Sometimes he would go into their homes and stay until they were well . . . or until they died. The fever was terrifying, striking with no warning. Those he could, he helped, but he could have been ten men and still there would have been the call—"Get Dr. Stuart!"

Aunt Lena, my grandmother's sister, said that her mother told them that he would come home—when he did come home—take a hot bath, change his underclothing and shirt, and then put his suit back on. She feared that the deadly germs were on that suit. Whether that's true or not, in the summer of 1876, little twelve-year-old Carrie was stricken with the fever. At first Dr. Stuart nursed her and then left instructions for his family to tend her while he visited his other patients. Finally, the fever was so great he would not leave her side.

Word was sent to him that his daughter Lil's baby had been taken ill with the fever. She was sure that if her father

48

would just come and care for the baby, the child would not die. But he could not leave his own child.

He could not save his little girl; he went to her funeral, and then that evening he rode to Greenville to see what he could do for his granddaughter. He was too late. The baby died later that night.

Death was all around them. Life became survival. Everything that could be done was done, all the precautions. Still Dr. Stuart made his rounds. Three weeks after Carrie died, he came down with the fever. At the same time, Colonel Griffin succumbed to the disease. Mary found herself caring for a household of children, her sick husband, and her sick father. Her mother helped as best she could, but Mary was afraid for her too. After all, Jemima Griffin was eighty-one years old. Mary feared also for the small children. The older children were a great help and consolation. But Mary feared for the newborn. How to nurse these sick ones and take care of those who were well?

At first John was able to direct her and the older children, explaining to them the process they were to go through to fight the fever. But he became weaker and weaker. Her father, too, at age eighty-eight was not fighting it well at all.

On October 4, 1876, Col. Larkin Griffin and Dr. John Alexander Stuart both died. Mary buried her father and her husband only weeks after she buried her daughter.

O mother of mine, how did you stand in that fall's wind? How did you put one foot in front of the other? Where did you get your strength?

I know the answer. She was the one in charge, and she did what had to be done. She turned to her church, to her faith, to her God. She could have raged against God for what happened to her, but that was not her way. Instead she called upon God to help her through the days that would come, to care for these children that God had seen fit to put in her care.

The loss was not only Mary's and the children's. When the community lost Dr. Stuart, they all grieved.

Somewhere between the hurt and the heart
    must come the decision
        to reject
          or cling to
            the faith.
Somewhere among the Why me?s and the anger
    and the screaming No!s and the soft incessant
        sobbing,
Somewhere in the aching persistent pain
    and the hopeless helpless nights,
Somewhere between the loud horror of what has
        happened
    and the quiet terror of silence
        comes
A turning away
        or a reaching out.
Somewhere between power and powerlessness
    comes
     the covenant cry
    and you either answer or you don't
    and you either live or you die.
"Therefore choose life,
    that you and your descendants may live."

No Matter
How Trampled

At this particular time, the South Carolina Presbytery was in session at the Rock Presbyterian Church in Ninety Six. Now I have no idea why the Presbytery would meet in Ninety Six in the midst of an epidemic of typhoid fever. I have no idea why they would meet at all, under the circumstances, but it's hard to stop Presbyterians from holding a meeting!

The next day, October 5, 1876, the South Carolina Presbytery attended the dual funeral of these two men who had shared a remarkable friendship over a number of years. My great-grandfather Stuart had been elected representative from the Rock Presbyterian Church to attend this meeting of Presbytery. My great-great-grandfather Griffin had been an ardent member of the Baptist church. The two caskets were placed side by side in front of the pulpit for the service.

The story was that one Sunday, some years back, Dr. Stuart had agreed to attend a service with Colonel Griffin in the Baptist church. When it came time to take communion, it was refused to Dr. Stuart. Colonel Griffin complained, saying that Dr. Stuart was the best man he had ever known and if the best man he knew was not good enough to take communion in the Baptist church, he would not darken the door again. He then began attending the Presbyterian church.

Colonel Griffin knew many of the men of the South Carolina Presbytery. A number of years previously, he had asked Dr. John McLees to preach his funeral in case he survived him. Dr. McLees had spent many hours in the Griffin home and had found Colonel Griffin to be a warm friend and a true Christian. In his sermon, Dr. McLees said of the close friendship of the two men, "They were lovely in their lives and in their death they were not divided."

Rev. J. O. Lindsay also spoke: "So teach us to number our days, that we may apply our hearts unto wisdom." He reminded the hearers of the uncertainty of death and of the importance of so taking account of the present moment that when death comes they might be able to meet it without fear; and he argued forcibly that "the fear of the LORD is the beginning of wisdom." He told the Presbytery that his heart was so full of sympathy and sorrow that he could not find words to speak of the deceased.

The last preacher was Rev. L. A. Broadus, "who also spoke feelingly of both the deceased" (according to the newspaper account of the dual funeral) and "gave their deathbed testimony as dying in the triumph of faith, and willing to depart and be with Christ."

Colonel Griffin's obituary said in part, "He was a man of great decision and integrity of character, and his unswerving devotion to duty was unsurpassed."

Dr. Stuart's obituary in the *Abbeville Press & Banner,* October 4, 1876, read as follows:

> Dr. Stuart was a man of refinement, education, and high moral worth, and was the most useful man in the community in which he lived. His portly frame, his manly carriage, his beaming eye, his radiant face, all plainly pointed him out as one of Nature's noblemen.

The following year Jemima died in her eighty-second year. I have no obituary. Surely there was one, but the family historians to whom I owe so much probably didn't think she was as important as Larkin. She saw most of her children precede her in death.

Who are my people? The sad truth is that, through the

generations since that first Scot put his foot on this soil, they have been a people who buried their children.

I've never understood that. The death of a child, no matter the age, before the parent, is somehow out of order. The pain strikes the heart like hot spews from the fire and embeds itself like an unrelenting leech.

I didn't have my loving done for you, Todd. . . .

Somewhere inside the human spirit
      hope lives.
No matter how trampled,
      how assaulted,
         how mocked our faith,
      hope lives.
For God's people have gone
      from crucifixion
         to the silence of the tomb
         to the resurrection morn.
Hope lives,
      for we've seen the face of God
      in the life
         and death
         and resurrection of Christ.

Heavy
on My Heart

The snow has stopped, at least for now, and over the early afternoon a peaceful silence has settled. I don't want to think of Todd, but Jemima and Mary are heavy on my heart. How did they deal with the pain? Did they pray for numbness? I have. Let me not think about it. Enough for today. Enough for a lifetime. . . .

Mary probably didn't have a chance to dwell on it except in the dark of night when the children were tucked in bed and the good friends had gone home and she found herself alone with her thoughts.

I hope nobody said to them, "At least you have other children." It's such an insensitive remark. Both of them had many other children, but if each person is a unique child of God, the grieving for one is unrelated to another.

My mother lost her first child, Margaret Barr, in childbirth. My mother told me about it often. She had very strong feelings about this daughter she knew for only nine months in her womb. I knew it was an ordeal for my mother just the way she would look when she would talk about it, just because years later she needed to talk about it. I listened and was terrified that one of my children would die just as birth held out its hand.

When Stuart was born and my mother was there for the birthing, there were two mothers who walked the halls together, two mothers who did not stop with the rest of us and gaze at the babies behind the glass, two mothers who would return home to decorated nurseries and little clothes that wouldn't be filled. I remember my mother saying as we looked at one of the blue babies who was slanted head down in its crib, "I'm glad that isn't our baby." I liked the way she claimed my children; she was right to do so. We all belong to each other.

When Todd was a baby, I would wake in the night and rush into the silence to see if he was all right. He would be lying on his back, sleeping peacefully. The doctor had told me to be sure to put him face down so he wouldn't choke. I had, and so had the nurses in the hospital, and then one would go in and find him on his back. Finally, on the fourth day of his little life, the nurses and I stood at the window in the nursery at the hospital and watched that little person push himself onto his back. The doctor had said nonsense, but we knew better!

The relief of seeing him breathing gently, the light of the moon catching him through the window, buoyed my spirit so I could return to my bed and sleep peacefully.

There is so much loving put into a child. I don't mean sacrificially. I never loved sacrificially. I loved and do love my children because they give me unending joy and because I can do no other. Of course, I've done things for them, but it's been no sacrifice to me; I've done things because I've wanted to do things, because I enjoy loving them. I could never give to them in any measure what they have given to me . . . and I have no control over that love; it just is. I think the ability to love is God-given. It's sometimes so painful a gift that you want to wish it away, but for the most part I thank God for it. I know this: I don't have to work up a love for my children (or my husband or my friends); it just is. It is no credit to me; it is God who said, You may love these children of mine, and you will be the one who will profit. There is no choice on my part.

And how I have been loved! One of the most treasured days of my life was in June of '82 (two months before Todd's death) when as we sat on the porch one evening, lingering over the supper table, Todd looked at me and said these incredible words: "How does it feel, Mom, to be adored by all four of your children?" No greater gift has any child ever given to his mother.

I look out at the snow, savoring the silence, wondering at the ways of life and death, and I think of my mother Mary Stuart that summer in 1876. I know that my mothers and my fathers stood in suffering many a time. I know they had the choice to fold or fight, and they fought: fought the daily barrage of life, fought against the unrelenting stabs of pain that come when you least expect them. They fought because we are a people of faith, and I have received my inheritance from my people and it is this: a yearning after faithfulness.

Who are your people? They are those who yearn to be faithful to the God who has been faithful to us. We are not always a people who understand the ways of God, but we are a people who have been claimed by God and we are a people who are grateful to God for that, and we are a people who try to be faithful in spite of our limited understanding.

The next year brought more fear to Mary Stuart. Both Thomas Calhoun and Mary Ann (whom we knew as Aunt Mame) fell to the fever. They were sick for weeks and Mary nursed them constantly.

One day a carload of ice came to Ninety Six and Mary Stuart bought a lot of it. It was packed in sawdust. When no one was in the room Thomas, too weak to walk, climbed out of bed and crawled over to the ice and pulled the blankets back from it, and when Mary came in he was lying on the floor, licking the ice. After that he got better. Soon Mary Ann got better, too. Mary Stuart's children were well!

Jesus wept.
It was as simple
          and as complicated
                    as that.
He wept.

He wept
   and in his weeping,
     he joined himself forever
      to those who mourn.
He stands now throughout all time,
   this Jesus weeping,
     with his arms about the weeping ones:
"Blessed are those who mourn, for they shall be
     comforted."
He stands with the mourners,
   for his name is God With Us, Immanuel.
Jesus wept.

Now That Was
a Christian Man!

In December of 1886, Mary Stuart moved her children to Greenville. The family lived on Washington Street, and it was there that Thomas Walter Barr called upon Ella Du-Barry Stuart. They were married on October 17, 1887. She was twelve years younger than he was. He didn't marry until he could afford a family. He wanted to marry someone with the same Christian ideals as the Barrs. And Ella DuBarry was the perfect choice.

My grandfather Barr was a heating and plumbing contractor in Greenville. He was a good businessman, an honest and hardworking man who was anxious to bring up his children in the nurture and admonition of the Lord. The family attended the First Presbyterian Church of Greenville, that same feeble colony that had been supported initially by Major McCann and Carmel Church. He was an elder and a respected man in the community.

My grandfather had the first Ford franchise in Greenville. His own car was a little red Ford with a rumble seat. He also had the dealership for other automobiles such as Reo and Hupmobile and Maxwell. There were no driver's licenses in those days, and my father learned to drive when he was a child by just getting into the car and starting off.

My father has such fond memories of his uncle Thomas. He was a favorite with the whole family. He never married because when his father, Dr. Stuart, died, he had the responsibility of caring for his widowed mother and all the little brothers and sisters. He was an example to my father of an unselfish and kindly man who always came to the defense of the children. Each of his sisters who had a son named one of them Tom after this brother who was so adored by them all. In fact, my father tried to teach his uncle Tom (for whom he had been named) how to drive. They got into Aunt Ella Gus's car, but when Uncle Tom backed up he dented the fender. My father exclaimed, "What are you going to tell Aunt Ella Gus?" Uncle Tom replied, "We'll just take it to Uncle Lark to fix it." They did, and he did, and Aunt Ella Gus was none the wiser. But Uncle Tom never learned to drive.

One summer Uncle Tom gave my father a job working on his farm, so my father moved in. One evening at the dinner table, young Thomas was enjoying himself devouring a number of delicious biscuits with plenty of butter and homemade jelly. Unfortunately, his capacity for biscuit-eating did not escape the eye of his vinegar-tongued Aunt Ella Gus. "Tom eats that jelly as if it comes in barrels," she announced. My father was terribly embarrassed, but right away Uncle Tom came to the rescue. "That's the way to eat it, isn't it, boys?" (He always called them "boys," whether there was one nephew or a group of them.) My father has been grateful ever since.

We pass on our faith by living it just as surely as by telling it. The best telling is the living of it. And when we make our children feel bad about themselves, we aren't passing on our stories. We're telling bad news instead of the Good News. This uncle was an agent of good news. He lived his faith and passed it on to the children in the family many a time. When my father and Heather and I went to the cemetery in Ninety Six that day, my father looked at his uncle Tom's grave and said to me, "Now that was a Christian man!" I looked at my father and I knew that behind those words was a faith that had passed from this man, Thomas Calhoun Stuart, to his namesake, my father. We are in so many ways made up of those who come before us. We are indebted to those who care enough to tell us that we are a people of God and that as such we are valued and prized. It's such a little thing to give to our children—to tell them they are cherished—but sometimes in the family life we are led astray by the siren call of success and we somehow don't have time to tell them our faith stories.

Sometimes I wonder, If we don't tell them, who will? Just as family stories get lost if they're not told, our faith will be lost to our children if we don't "bring them up in the nurture and admonition of the Lord." If we leave faith nurturing entirely to the ministers and the church school teachers, how will our children know that our faith is our life? If we don't live what we say we believe, how will they know we are a people of God? My great-uncle Tom Stuart intentionally made my father feel good and not bad. Families can do that for you: They can make you feel good about yourself or they can make you feel bad. The Barrs and the Stuarts generally do a good job of making their children feel valued—feel good about themselves. A child who feels good about himself or herself will be an adult able to make the world a little better. On the gravestone of Thomas Calhoun Stuart are these words:

HE SERVED GOD AND HIS FELLOWMEN

Simple, but to the point. He lived what he had been taught, and he taught it to the children.

It was faith that made Noah go into the unknown
        amid the jeering crowd
        against the conventional wisdom.

It was faith that made Noah
        prepare for rain that was not predicted
        and hold a two-by-two parade into the ark.

It was faith that kept Noah going
        through a flood the likes of which
        the world had never seen,
        the wrath of God raining on the faithless.

Because of faith, Noah collected promises
        on dry land
        where first of all he and his family
            knelt
                and gave thanks to God
        who made a new promise: Never again!

Offering Up
Their Joy

When Todd was four, he took to church one Sunday morning a glorious balloon we had acquired the day before. It was orange with pink stripes and it was oversized and wonderful. But the teacher didn't see what it meant to him, didn't take the time to make him feel good about having brought it. When he carried it home and told me that the teacher had said "We don't bring balloons to church," I had to work furiously to undo the damage. What do we think we're doing to little hearts and little minds that are offering up their joy? It's not the faith we're passing on, but our own frustrations and anxieties of our "adult" world.

It's so easy to fall into the trap of letting the rules control us, especially when we're tired and put upon and have fifteen little wiggly children to teach in fifty minutes. We do teach them, but sometimes we teach them to dislike church because the teacher's irritable or a stickler for rules that have nothing to do with our faith stories.

I showed Heather the picture of her great-great-grandfather Barr surrounded by his family and asked her if she could pick out her great-grandfather, my father's father. She took a quick look, said that was easy, and put her finger on Thomas Walter Barr. She said it was the eyes. He was a handsome young man, that oldest son of George and

Martha Jane Barr, and Heather's right: I've seen those eyes, even though I never saw my grandfather.

My grandfather was the father of eight. He was, perhaps, not as sensitive to the feelings of little children as was Uncle Tom, but he wanted his children to grow up knowing that faith was an everyday affair. He expected his family to live out that faith even if you were a little six-year-old boy who skipped school.

My father had seen a red lantern in a store that he desperately wanted to buy. He arranged to spend the night with a cousin who lived up the street, and as they started out for school he told the cousin he needed to stop by the house for something he'd forgotten. The cousin went on, and my father walked to town and made his purchase. Then he had the rest of the morning on his hands. His mistake was that after wandering around looking in store windows, he went to the store operated by his older brothers. Of course, they told his father and Papa appeared within minutes. Into the car they went. When they rounded the corner near the school, my father, hoping to stall a little longer, threw his hat out of the car. His father told him to get it and, after the boy retrieved it, drove the car to their house and, behind the garage, gave Thomas a switching (with a freshly cut switch) he never forgot. Thomas was then delivered to the schoolroom where, much to his surprise, the teacher did not add to his punishment but showed him to his seat and continued with her teaching.

Talking about the incident years later, my father said he thought his own father had overdone it a bit, and he had been grateful ever since to the teacher who sensed that Thomas had learned his lesson. The Barrs were a responsible family, and Thomas's responsibility at age six was to be in school. He never skipped school again. In fact, even when he got to seminary and attendance was optional, he made every class!

Grandfather Barr could be strict and demanding, but he could provide his family with a lot of happy memories. He would take any number of Barr children on excursions, his children and his brothers' and sisters' children. The year my father was born, 1904, Grandfather Barr took off with several of the children to see the World's Fair in St. Louis. Just a few streets from where I live now are the fairgrounds where my grandfather and my uncles and aunts feasted their eyes on the wonders of the world. My grandfather instilled in his children a sense of adventure.

My father was the youngest of the boys and seventh of the eight children, but since my grandfather believed in the experience of excursions, he took my father by train to Charleston to pick up a car. My father was only five or six and thrilled to be going with Papa all by himself on a train ride. It was a night train, and Papa, exhausted from his day's work, began to doze. Each time the train stopped, which was at every little junction, young Thomas woke his papa to tell him that the train was pulling in to a new place. Papa would thank him and doze off again until the next stop.

Another time, Thomas discovered in the Sears, Roebuck catalog an Indian suit that he wanted Papa to buy for him. Papa was working diligently on his paper work in the parlor, but Thomas hounded him until he stopped and placed an order for the Indian suit. Papa was a man who made it clear to his children that he cared the world for them, whether he expressed it in a switching or in a great deal of patience on a night train to Charleston or in ordering an Indian suit in the midst of pressing business.

The punishment for skipping school did little to squelch my father's spirit. There was all sorts of trouble to get into, with four sisters and three brothers and a host of cousins, and something tells me little Thomas didn't even need the others!

Our all-time favorite is the story of the day my father went to school after seeing an Oriental movie. He was very impressed with the empress and the fact that every time her servants left the room, they would bow and fold their hands in a subservient attitude and back out of the room. Well, because Thomas went to see this movie, he did not have time to do his homework. When he arrived at school and the other pupils placed their homework in a pile on the teacher's desk, Thomas just went on by, but the teacher saw him and asked him where his homework was. He confessed that he had not done it and she made him write on the blackboard one hundred times: *I will not fail to do my homework.* When he had finished, the teacher was writing some instructions on the blackboard and Thomas bowed his head, folded his hands, and backed all the way to his seat. The class was in an uproar. When the teacher turned around she asked them what was so funny. No one answered. There was silence interspersed with giggles. Finally she said, "All right, you will all stay in from recess except Thomas, who was the only one who did not laugh." He went out by himself!

It occurs to me that, as a family, we laugh a lot. We all love the stories of "Thomas in trouble." I guess you could say our family preaches that laughter is a part of our faith. After all, God made us to laugh.

If it's anything my mother did not like, it was piosity. She resented the stereotypical portrayal of Christians as long-faced, dour, judgmental people. It certainly isn't biblical, for we are called to be cheerful and joyful. Actually, I've noticed lately how many people who have experienced profound grief or pain seem to be able to rebound laughing. Their love of life and the depth of their faith surface magnificently. Instead of cursing their lot, they turn all that energy into living faithfully and abundantly, and their laughter is sweet to my ears.

All of us good church people know the story
        of how Joshua "fit the battle of Jericho."
But few of us remember Rahab.
The Sunday school lessons
        avoid   ignore   remain silent about
            this woman who (along with God)
            made the whole strategy possible.
Sometimes God's choices leave us
        a little baffled, a little embarrassed.
Why a harlot?
Surely there was in Jericho some goodworks woman
        who had lived a nearly saintly life . . .
                        BUT
The churched and the chaste
        are not always God's choices.
God reads hearts rather than position papers
        on the state of our virtue.
It always makes me a little nervous
        when God makes these unlikely choices.
Perhaps we in the church should appoint a task force
        to be sure that we're the Wall Tumblers
            rather than the Wall Builders.

Paris Mountain

By the time my father was born, the house on Paris Mountain had been in existence for eight years. My grandfather built it in 1896 so that the family would have a happy place to spend their summer days. It was hot in the Greenville sun, and only a few miles away up on the mountain it was definitely cooler.

I never saw the house, but I saw the steps that my father built when he was a boy. The boys were in charge of fixing the steps, and with the traffic of the large family plus their grandfather's family plus the cousins and uncles and aunts, the steps seemed to need constant attention. My father decided to solve the problem by building concrete steps. He did.

When the house burned down, the only remaining evidence that there had been a house was the steps that Thomas built. Years later my father took his family to Paris Mountain, and there on the vast property were the steps. They are still there, and the property is owned today by a Barr, the granddaughter of my father's sister, Lucille. I take a lot of comfort in that, for through my father's stories I can hear the laughter echoing off Paris Mountain.

I have heard many a story about the fun on Paris Mountain. I think my grandfather Barr knew what he was doing when he built that house, a place where his family could grow in the summers in the values that he and my grandmother believed in because of their faith, their own up-bringing.

Now I wouldn't want you to think that Paris Mountain was a place for just hymn singing and Bible-reading. There are many stories of the shenanigans that went on upon that mountain, and the Barrs were at the bottom of a lot of them.

Many of the stories were told about my great-grandfather and how he ingeniously met the everyday problems of life.

On Paris Mountain, Great-grandfather would fiddle on his violin in the afternoons on the porch. He was a good musician and had in the past gathered his family for many a hymn sing. My father said his playing would become quite funereal right before dinner and liven up afterward.

On this porch my great-grandfather would watch the thunderstorms. The valley, which could be clearly seen because my grandfather kept the trees topped for the view, looked as though toys had been sprinkled over it—toy farms and toy automobiles and toy horses pulling toy carts, even a toy train.

When the electrical storms came, everybody took shelter in the house and stayed away from the windows, but not my great-grandfather. I was in a storm once on Paris Mountain when my family and my mother and father were visiting my cousins, Ella and Frank Kemble. It was incredible: lightning bolts the likes of which I'd never seen before. We stood at the window, protected, and even then shivered at the might of the crackling and the display of radiance that came with the lightning. It was in this type of storm that Great-grand-father Barr stayed on the porch, glorying in the spectacle of it. I'm attracted to storms myself, but I do have an honest fear and don't defy the bolts to come near me. My great-grandfather, however, wanted a ringside seat for the fire-works of God!

But then this man was not afraid of anything, according to his grandchildren. In the middle of the main room in their grandfather's house was a hole. My father and his brothers and sisters loved the story of that hole.

"Early in the morning after it was light, Grandfather, half

69

asleep, heard a suspicious hissing sound. He slept with the front door open, and through the door a rattlesnake had come. Seeing the source of the hissing, Grandfather caught hold of the handle he had put beside his bed and, raising himself with the other hand, got his trusted rifle which always hung in the rack beside the bed. Sitting up in bed, he shot the snake, which had to be dead, for Grandfather never missed. The marksman calmly replaced the rifle, settled down in bed, and continued his morning nap. But only for an hour, for he said that within an hour there would be a second rattler following the path of the first."

I think I would have gotten up, although when I was a girl, I awoke one night to see my brother Tom on his hands and knees beside my bed. "What are you doing?" I'm sure I screamed at him.

"I'm just looking for my snake," he answered, "but it's all right. I've found him under your bed."

It wasn't a rattler, but it was close enough. My brother Tom, a scientist, worked at the children's museum in Nashville during his high school years and often had snakes home for a visit. He was supposed to keep them on the third floor, but sometimes they wandered. Actually, I preferred the snakes to the bats.

Our lives are made up of
  silence and star.
Our faith sings
  even in the silence
Because we have seen the
  Bright and Morning Star.

I Will Never
Finish Life

My father remembers his grandfather very fondly. Of course, he never knew his grandfather Stuart and felt very fortunate that his grandfather Barr was around for so long. In fact, he was very fortunate to have all the family that he did have and to have them near at hand. Today's families are scattered the country over, and closeness is often hard to come by. I try hard to keep in touch with my brothers and my sister and we do fairly well, but it's usually by mail. It is very difficult to get us all together. We have to plan far in advance. My father takes little trips to South Carolina to see his family. He's always been close to them. There are just three left now, the three youngest: Aunt Mary and my father and Aunt Monte. Uncle Walter just died this past year.

In November I was in Aunt Monte's home in New Jersey. I've been there three or four times in the past few years. The first time I went after not seeing her for years, we sat down together and in ten minutes were talking just like we'd always talked. I love to visit with Aunt Monte. She loves me so beautifully.

My father remembers the time that little Margaret—Aunt Monte—was lost. The circus was in town and Margaret disappeared. The adults feared she had been kidnapped by the circus people. What he remembers most about the incident was Aunt Harriet, sitting in the kitchen by the window with big tears running down her dark face, and the joy in her eyes when Margaret was found, none the worse for wear.

All the children learned love from Aunt Harriet. She was a Christian who took her Christianity seriously. Her faith was a daily affair, and she expressed it by doing things for other people.

She was a cook, a marvelous cook, and somehow or another she would cater to each and every one in that large family. Everyone had his or her waffle fixed a special way. Of course, she knew that good eating was good for you and she wanted to do what was good for you, so if you didn't eat, she translated that into "bad." "Mr. Hal is a Christian; he eats everything on his plate."

I love it!

Aunt Harriet was always interested in the special projects or goals of the children. She would advise and help them to carry out their schemes or dreams.

When my father was twelve, he decided he wanted to become a missionary. He had no hope of leaving immediately for Africa, so he set his evangelistic zeal upon the black children who were Aunt Harriet's grandchildren.

"One Sunday afternoon we met, equipped with literature my brother-in-law, a Presbyterian minister, had obtained for me free. One solid piece of literature was the Westminster Shorter Catechism. In the Sunday school we attended it was the standard text of study and, if we could, we were expected to memorize its theological words and answer all the questions at one sitting. For this Herculean task, which few to my knowledge performed, you received a Bible from the Christian Observer with a letter of commendation from 'Dear Mr. Converse.'

"I still can't remember how many sessions of this school were held. I do remember the authority of Aunt Harriet, which she did not hesitate to wield reinforced with her walking stick. One can imagine how inspiring I was to the black boys my own age as I tried to teach them the Shorter Catechism. My zeal flagged with my lack of success, and instead of actual work I dreamed of the fields of Africa, where I could be a missionary hero after the fashion of David Livingstone."

It seems easy to confuse action for faith. My father admits to being smitten with an evangelistic zeal that was not well directed. A faith that matured changed that direction. At that time it was Aunt Harriet who was the evangelist.

I myself worked very hard to learn the Child's Catechism. I was six years old when I received my New Testament. I could hear the remarks of the men and women who attended this church school event: "Smart little thing, isn't she?" "Only six years old." "Her father and mother have done so well with her." "So delighted to have that Testament." Yes, I was delighted. I had worked hard, and no wonder, it would be mine, all mine. All those wonderful red letters. And that's what I read. Gleefully skipping over that boring black stuff, I read the words of Jesus, to myself and out loud. I confess that's why I learned the catechism—all those red, red letters.

I loved to read in bed when I was a child, and I still love to read in bed. It was the last thing I did before I went to sleep, but my mother didn't approve of the hour of my bedtime. I resorted to reading under the covers by flashlight, and she still caught me. Finally, I hit upon an idea. When she entered the room and said, "I told you no reading at this hour," I very piously drew my Bible from under the covers and said, "Well, I just wanted so to finish this chapter." She said, "It won't work; turn out the light." Heathen mother!

Fortunately, we do mature in our faith, but it takes years of nurture, years of parents' patiently answering questions, teachers' answering questions, years of being asked questions by those adults who take the time to care to ask.

In times to come, when our children ask us, will we be ready? Of all our children, I've had the deepest theological discussions with Todd. I've done a lot of soliloquies and I hope some of that penetrated, but it is with Todd that both

Don and I struggled to answer the volume of theological questions he had.

One day in the spring before he died, he asked me if I still missed Gladys, my mother. I said yes, that still I grieved for her and she had been gone five years. I commented to him that something would happen and I would think, Oh, I've got to write Gladys, before I realized, No need now. Todd said that if he were to die before I did, he didn't want me to be sad; that I could know he was happy, for all his questions would be answered and he would see the face of God.

I will never finish life,
And it will never finish me.
Return to it its seeds, its soil,
For you and I as the plants and God as the toiler
Work together toward the common goal:
To love one another. . . .
Ever love to never end.
I want, I feel, to kiss my God.
                              —Todd Calhoun Weems

Dan-Dan

On January 10, 1915, when my father was only eleven, my grandfather Barr died, aged fifty-seven. On February 7, not even a month later, my great-grandfather Barr died at seventy-nine. Out of the life of my father, just eleven, went the two stalwart men of the family.

Of course, his grandfather was getting old, but not too old to lead those excursions through the woods on Paris Mountain, not too old to repair a boy's rifle, not too old to tell his stories of the wonderful exploits of his dog Prince, not too old to fiddle on the porch or tell a boy how to measure the distance of lightning. But his grandfather was no more, and the boy's loss was great.

And Papa . . . what would any of them do without Papa? He was the head of the family since Grandfather had retired. He was strong and smart and vital and he shouldn't have died and left them. He was the one with the ideas; he was the entrepreneur; he was the one who could build and support them and hire his brothers and his sons to help. He was the one they depended on, and he was gone.

My grandmother, my precious Dan-Dan (nicknamed that because one of the grandchildren who came before me couldn't say Grandmother) was alone with eight children. Of course, had she been more assertive, had it been another time, today, she could have insisted on holding on to the property, but Grandfather's brother settled with her. She was very frugal and made ends meet as best she could. She set about to nurture her children, to educate them as best she could, and to give them the good Christian upbringing she wanted for them. She had family—both Barrs and Stuarts were supportive—but still, in an age when women had few rights, my grandmother had a very hard time of it. The older boys were on their own, but how could she give to the younger children what they would have had from their father?

My father had a real financial struggle getting through college and then through seminary. That's another Barr characteristic: I can do it. It will be hard, but I can do it. And he did. Of course, he had help, but I remember my mother telling me that when he was in seminary he went without food for a few days so that he could send her a box of Valentine chocolates. She saved that box and I have it now, filled to the brim with their love letters.

My father chose a good church-related college in the South, Davidson College. While he was there, he wrote a short story for the school paper. To quote from the Greenville paper of the time:

> Davidson College, N.C. Dec. 20 (Special)—For the present at least the miniature rebellion which has rocked the campus of Davidson College for the past several weeks is ended: a new editor has been elected for the college magazine, replacing C. F. Monk, who was deposed as editor because of an objectionable story which appeared in the first quarterly issue of the magazine this year, and all is peace and harmony in collegiate circles here. But still the campus is wondering who won in the controversy—students or faculty? That is the question.
>
> ### *"Dim Morning"* Story
>
> Following the appearance of the first quarterly issue of the magazine this year, there arose quite a squabble about a story "Dim Morning" which was published under the nom de plume "Adrian Prevost." The story centered around the portrayal of the modernisms at a college house party, apparently written more or less as a protest against "petting" and other familiarities of the younger generation. C. F. Monk, the edi-

tor of the magazine and one of the most popular men on the campus, was haled before the faculty despite the protest of the student body.

And then to cap the controversy, Thomas C. Barr, of Greenville, S.C., who, it is said in reliable circles, wrote "Dim Morning," using the nom de plume of "Adrian Prevost," has been elected editor of the college publication, from which post Monk was deposed because he allowed the story to go into the columns of the magazine.

Students Protest

When the students learned that Monk had been asked to resign there was talk of discontinuing the magazine. But the little rebellion was quieted by the steadying influence of the deposed editor. Barr was elected editor through the recommendation of Monk, it is said. And thus, with an editor deposed because he published a story, the man who wrote the story gets the editorship.

Is Greenville Boy

Thomas C. Barr, mentioned in the above news dispatch, is a son of Mrs. Ella Barr of this city, and has many friends here who will be interested in the announcement that he has been elected editor of the Davidson magazine. Mr. Barr is one of the best-known and most popular Greenville young men who are away at college. He is a senior at the North Carolina institution, and is very popular with the students.

For the first time in the magazine's history there was a sellout! Buyers clamored for more stories by "Adrian Prevost." And the student body had a sense of humor. They elected my father, who had written the story, as editor! He accepted—graciously, I'm sure, and with the blessing of the deposed editor. But the faculty was furious. My father was obviously contumacious!

I've always loved my father's sense of humor. When we're together there's a lot of laughter. His life has been a significant one where faith is concerned, and yet he's never taken himself so seriously that he can't enjoy himself. He would agree with Isaac Watts and Mr. McGill of the Indiantown dancing incident: "Religion never was designed to make our pleasures less."

My grandmother was still trying to instill Christian virtues in her children during the wild and crazy days of the Roaring Twenties. In a letter dated May 29, 1924, she writes to her son at Davidson:

Dear Thomas,

Your letter several days ago made me very happy. I was feeling rather badly and it helped to cheer me very much. I surely am glad you appreciate your home and I hope you always will. Papa and I tried to make a happy Christian home, but I feel sometimes I've failed, especially since he is not here to help me. My boys seem to love their home more than the girls, but I hope as the years go by, and they see the real value of things, they will realize what I've tried to do. They think it terrible that I don't want them to dance and play cards, but I had hoped they would be interested in things more worth-while. Margaret is having a little party tomorrow night on her birthday, and they want me to let them dance, but I cannot conscientiously let them do so. I do hope she will soon get interested in something besides boys. As to what I said to you about girls, I've forgotten, but boys don't usually fall in love with girls that possess so many virtues. You can watch out, tho, and tell a good deal about them by the things they like, their taste, etc., and from their parents if you happen to know them. I have seen frivolous girls that didn't seem to have a serious thought turn out to make splendid wives. Above all things I'd want to marry a *Christian,* for life is hard at best and unless we have that faith, trust, and hope in God to help us, we can do little. I trust you'll get a good Christian girl some-day, and one who is attractive and congenial and will be willing to help you in your work. I hope you will get one who is much smarter and will make a better home than I have done. I appreciate more than I can tell you what you said about Papa and me. Yes, he surely did love his home and children. He has often told me what fine children we had and how he hoped they would grow up to be good and useful men and women in the world and in the church. I know he would be happy to know you have given your life to the

80

ministry for he always wanted one of his boys to be a preacher, and he always thought so much of you, and was so proud of you. I am glad you will soon be home with us. Know you will enjoy hearing Little Margaret talk. Hope you have a nice time at commencement. Would like to see the girl you spoke of, am glad you tried to get her interested in better things, and hope she will. Have to stop now. Much love from me and the others,

Mother

In that letter, my grandmother summed up the hope that the Barrs and the Stuarts have carried in their hearts and passed her faith to her children. What better epitaph could we want?

I loved it when Dan-Dan was coming to see us. She traveled from one child's home to the next, and we looked forward to her visits with such joy. She was not the kind of grandmother who would bring you big surprises; she simply could not afford it. But she always brought each of us some little treasure, picked out for that child. My mother looked forward to her visits as much as we did. Dan-Dan would darn all the socks, do all the sewing that was stacking up at our house. My mother had never learned to sew. She didn't need to; she was a lawyer and a writer.

I wish I had asked Dan-Dan some of the questions about her family that may now be lost forever, but at that time I was more interested in just talking to her. I used to love to go in when she was getting ready for bed and watch her let down her hair. It was long and a white white that is matched only by my father's. How they keep it so white, I still don't know. I've seen yellowed white hair so often, but my grandmother's was like snow upon her head. Her skin was amazingly smooth, and she used to let us cuddle up to her and nuzzle against that soft, flawless skin. She washed her face and put cream on it (she never wore makeup). Then she let that white hair fall and she brushed it a hundred times. Every time she'd come I'd go into my hairbrushing regime —a hundred times every night—but my hair was thin and

81

short and tended to wave and brushing just didn't hold its glamour once Dan-Dan was gone.

After she brushed her hair, she would hang her corset and her undergarments, some of which I don't understand to this day, in the closet. She'd already hung her dress properly as soon as she took it off and would be wearing a soft flannel nightgown and a robe that smelled of roses and Dan-Dan. Then she would open up her little gray-striped traveling case and get her Bible and read it out loud to me . . . only because I asked. I can see those stiff fingers groping to turn the page. Her voice was soft and lovely, and I looked at her and loved her mightily. I still love her. She was a child of God who passed her faith on to her children and her grandchildren. Her words are the words that I would want my children to hear: *Life is hard at best and unless we have that faith, trust, and hope in God to help us, we can do little.*

Oh, Dan-Dan! I still see you fall at our home in Nashville on a visit. I see you grimace—not cry out in a loud voice, I never heard you raise your voice—you grimace and the ambulance comes and you are taken away and I am terrified. Later my father calls; your hip is broken. The doctors pin it. After a while you are doing better and you come home, not to your home in Greenville but to our home in Nashville.

It is I who am asked to sleep with you in the dining room where we made a temporary bedroom so you wouldn't have to go upstairs. It is I who am awakened in the dark of the night by your voice calling me. I rush to you and find you wringing wet and hot. The ambulance again in the night, and when my parents have left for the hospital, I wander back to your bed and see the wet spot where your head had lain. I touch it and long to see your long white hair upon the pillow.

I remember walking to the hospital every afternoon after school and sitting quietly in Dan-Dan's room. I was not an assertive girl, but when I saw the orderlies in the hospital changing the bed one day, roughly and quickly jerking my

82

Dan-Dan around as though she were a piece of meat, I yelled at them to be careful. They looked at me, astonished, and said, "She doesn't feel it; she doesn't know what's going on." I screamed at them, "*I* know what's going on!"

One afternoon I heard Dan-Dan call my name, and I thought she was coming out of the coma. I got up and went to her and I saw the most ethereal look come over her face and then she said, "Oh, Mama, Mama . . . Sis Lil. . . . Oh, Bessie . . . Brother Tom. . . ." All the names were of people who had died long ago.

I don't know how we get to heaven, but wouldn't it be just like God to arrange that we be met and brought in by those we love and who love us? If that's the way it is, my Dan-Dan was on her way. During the night she died. It was April 4, 1951. I was seventeen.

We took her back to Greenville to be buried next to my grandfather. We went in a caravan because my Aunt Lil was there and Aunt Monte and we couldn't get everybody in the car. I did some of the driving around those mountains. We were supposed to follow my father's lead and did most of the time, but my family always loved a good laugh and we decided we would pass my father and his carload, probably full of boys and menfolk. When we passed we waved and laughed outrageously for hours. That night, after arriving and greeting all the other kin, we laughed ourselves sick. We had all been so tense, and after Dan-Dan died, every little thing that happened seemed hilarious. I know we were just letting down after all the stress. Nobody felt guilty about it; everybody was happy to be together. The only thing we felt bad about was that we couldn't have come together during her lifetime: all her children and their children and her sisters and other family. Families today gather for funerals and weddings, but we find life too pressing to gather for fun or maybe for reaffirmation of faith!

My grandmother had little to leave to any of her children. Actually some of them had been supporting her, helping her out as best they could. Somehow my father knew how

I felt about Dan-Dan, and he handed me her little gray-striped traveling case. I look at it now and I can almost see her fingers opening it and bringing out that Bible. I was also given the mirror that she kept in the case to see herself brush her long white hair.

I am the daughter of I AM.
You are a child of God.
We are the family of God
          and there is at our family table
     a place for every child of God,
          and bread and wine enough for all.
What we have to do is send out
          the invitations.

Kidnappers Foiled

My mother said she was terribly anxious when she was going to meet Dan-Dan. After all, Gladys was a Yankee girl from Albany, New York, and all my father's family were entrenched in southern tradition. She needn't have been afraid. Gladys was from a good Christian family and had the same yearning after faith that my father did. In fact, their love letters often mention some theological problem or another.

My mother was one of the few women lawyers in the 1920s. She was (as my husband describes her) "larger than life." She was a person of enormous energy, talent, and intellect.

As a girl she was used to finding her name and often her picture in the paper for one thing after another. She accumulated many awards and was quite popular in high school and college. She attended Albany Law School and as a freshman was elected president of the class, the first woman president.

I have an Albany newspaper clipping captioned *Girl President of Law School Frosh Foiled Kidnappers.*

Hearing she was to be kidnapped by the junior class as fitting mete for the president of the freshman class at Albany Law School, Miss Gladys Hutchinson, first girl president of the law school class, outwitted the bold, bad upper classmen last night and attended the freshmen's get-together at St. Andrew's Hall, unmolested. How did she do it?

Miss Hutchison peeped out of the window of her home in Pine Hills and saw mysterious figures lurking in the darkness. So she put on a suit of men's clothes, tucked her blond curls under a cap, and set out. The juniors, waiting for a young lady with all the frills of femininity, let her pass. She reached the hall in time to change her costume and preside.

Miss Hutchison is the daughter of Professor Hutchison of the State College.

Former State Senator Frank L. Wiswall, the speaker of the evening, complimented the girl president on her courage and wit.

At a later date, there is a picture of my mother and the caption is: *Albany Miss Has No Fear of Wicked Juniors and Plots. She'll Face 'Em on Their Own Ground at Law School Prom Friday.*

She's the first girl president of the freshman class at the Albany Law School and the naughty juniors have laid many plots against her safety, but Gladys W. Hutchison is going to lead the freshman delegation to the annual junior prom which takes place Friday at the Ten Eyck.

When the first freshman dinner took place last fall, juniors attempted to capture Miss Hutchison and prevent her from speaking, but she outwitted them by leaving her home donned in a boy's makeup.

I remember Mother—
    not cleaning and polishing,
      though the house did sparkle,
    not scrubbing and sweeping,
      though we all pitched in.
I remember Mother creating fun!
  When Halloween came,
    our mother was the witch
      that had us squealing in her parlor!
  When Thanksgiving came our mother was so thankful
      for us
    that she went out and
      found people who had no children to be grateful
      for
      and invited them to our feast.
        I forget when she cooked;
      I suppose it was when we were laughing in the
        kitchen.
When Christmas came,
  our mother, who couldn't sew,
  always had a friend who thanked her effusively
    for the privilege of sewing our pageant costumes,
  and we always seemed to know that the greatest
    present of all was the Christ.
When Good Friday came
  our mother fed us hot cross buns
    and told us of Jesus who died on a cross.
On Easter morning we would have new clothes
    even when we couldn't afford them
  because new clothes reminded her of resurrection.
We were fortunate because our mother
  the lawyer and the writer
    was never as busy as other mothers
      who disappeared to clean kitchens and closets.

Our mother always had time
  to play a game of Monopoly
  or to discuss the world situation
  with seven-year-olds.
Our mother taught us many things,
  but the best thing was
  that being Christian is a lifetime joy.

A Call
to the Ministry

My father had gone from Davidson College in North Carolina to Union Theological Seminary in New York—not Richmond, but New York. I asked him just this year how on earth he ever landed in New York with his southern heritage. He told me that, when he was a senior at Davidson, various representatives came to talk to the students who were considering seminary. My father said he got more and more anxious as he heard these men talk about the ministry. He knew he was in trouble when he heard their very conservative remarks. He was really very upset about it and wondered if he should even go to seminary. He was very much influenced by an article he had read in *Forum* magazine. The author was Dr. Henry Sloane Coffin, president of Union, and it was entitled "Why I Am a Presbyterian." He said he was a Presbyterian because he had been born one. My father knew that was why he was a Presbyterian. The article was quite broad-based and ecumenical. The most important thing was being a Christian and living out that faith in the best way possible. Wasn't that what my father had been feeling? He was determined he would attend Union.

It wasn't easy because finances were very tight. At one point he felt he was going to have to leave seminary because he just couldn't make a go of it even with the money his mother sent and the money he got from the church where he worked in New Jersey and from his summer job at the First Presbyterian Church in New York. Dr. Coffin interceded and got him an additional job in a Reformed church.

Dr. Coffin seemed to take a special interest in my father, which delighted my father greatly. Dr. Coffin would often see him walking through the halls after a class and say, "Tom, you look pale. Let's take a walk." They would walk along Riverside Drive and talk theology.

By the time my father graduated, he wanted to keep his promise to himself of returning to ministry in the South, but his head and heart were full of the teachings of Dr. Coffin and also of Dr. Harry Emerson Fosdick. Could he be of use in a pulpit in the South? My father simply did not share the racial prejudice of so many Southerners. Nor did he share some of the narrow theological concepts that he had met while he was in college. He was not a troublemaker; he didn't like confrontation. He did feel a very strong sense of what the Christian faith was all about, and he has always preached that Christianity must tie into contemporary life to be effective and legitimate.

In the absence
of a burning bush
or a blinding light
or a voice that claims us,
how does one know
for sure
that it is God who is calling?
Of course, the question could be asked:
How does one know anything for sure?
Perhaps this is where faith comes in
and hope
and love
and prayer without ceasing. . . .
I do know
that when the hand of God
is laid on the shoulder of our lives
somehow
we do know.
We are even given the boldness to say,
"Here am I. Send me."

21 North Pine Avenue

The snow has started again and I get up to poke the fire. It's burned for a long time actually. I built a good fire; I'm surprised. I walk into the kitchen to put the kettle on for tea. While it's heating, I look out the back, and on the porch is the small statue of St. Francis. I bought it at the garage sale of a friend one time. Not very Presbyterian, perhaps, but I have a special place in my heart for St. Francis. My mother wrote about him. The summer following my senior year in high school she took me to Europe and we researched St. Francis.

The St. Francis on my back porch is wearing a green ski cap. I laugh and know that David is around. I hadn't heard him come in, and I don't hear him now. On the table is the grocery list, and in David's handwriting is added: Birdseed.

Yes, the birds need to be fed.

David has always been the one closest to St. Francis, to the birds, to the animals. He reminds me of his great-grandfather David Hutchison, for whom he is named. He too fed the birds and the squirrels and loved the dogs enormously.

My grandfather Hutchison was born in Arbroath, Scotland, in 1866. His father had been a sculptor in Edinburgh, but he had to give it up "as the dust from the stone made him ill." So he sought his fortune in Canada, where he became a contractor. He bought a farm in Victoria County twenty miles from Orillia because he thought that would be a good place for my grandfather to grow up. However, my grandfather didn't like farm life, and as soon as he was able he went to McGill University in Montreal.

When I was fourteen or fifteen, our family traveled to Orillia to see my grandfather's sister and her family. They farm there even today.

My mother was anxious to trace her genealogy, and at best it is sketchy. She could come up with nothing like the Barrs although she tried hard enough.

My great-grandfather was named James. I have a picture of him; he looks like an elf dressed up in fancy clothes.

After my grandfather graduated from McGill he was the principal of a school in Ontario for two years until he accumulated "funds" enough to return to Montreal and attend the Presbyterian College. The Hutchisons, too, were Presbyterian and they too often named their children after the fathers and mothers of our biblical faith.

In Montreal my grandfather met my grandmother. Exactly how they met, I'm not sure. He saw a picture of her on the society page of the paper. He told me that as soon as he saw that picture, he was determined she would be his wife. That picture hung for years in their dining room, testimony to their story.

When I was a child I used to stare at that picture: a young woman beautifully dressed in highly styled ivory gown, long kid gloves, fan with tassel, her hair swept up in the fashion of the day. Her waist was pinched, and she wore a beautiful gold locket with matching gold earrings with a stone inset. She was tall and regal. I had a hard time relating this young woman to the old woman who sat on a chair in the parlor.

Actually I avoided the parlor when I could manage it. My brothers and sisters and I would try to avoid being hugged to my grandmother's rather large bosom. She was so large and we were so small. Clutched to her I couldn't breathe. My mother always gave us a little lecture on the way to the house: "Give Grandfather a kiss on the porch." (His whiskers always made my skin red, but he was not a hugger; I could endure his greeting.) "Then go into the parlor and

94

give Grandmother a kiss." (I would have been happy to give her a kiss; it was the lingering bear hug, crushed to her bosom, that we dreaded.) I had the decency to feel guilty about it; I knew she had nothing to look forward to, sitting in that chair, day after day, and she was as sweet as she could be. I've thought about that since then. She adored us; she was loving us. She felt that overwhelming love that grandparents have for their grandchildren, an uncontrollable loving that is manifested in a lot of touching. We were *life* to her quiet day.

Another reason I avoided the parlor was that my grandmother would ask me to stand for what seemed interminable lengths of time as she twisted her wool around my two arms to make a ball of it. I've never liked standing still and didn't really appreciate the adventures of Stella Dallas that came daily over the radio.

I could never understand how my grandmother could sit in the parlor, day after day, knitting or reading or listening to Stella Dallas and all the preachers. That was her life really, that and her beloved David.

I've seen people smitten before, but never have I seen the adoration that my grandmother held for my grandfather, and he for her in a different way. He didn't look moony-eyed at her, but he catered to her every wish. He brought her tea and did the housework and later, when she "took to bed" for the rest of her life, he took her trays and brought her presents and loved her unconditionally. They had the greatest respect for each other. I don't think when he looked at her that he saw the old woman whom we saw. I think he saw the young girl on the society page of the paper, the young girl who had everything.

Near the debutante picture in the dining room was their wedding picture. My grandfather stood straight and tall, at five feet eight inches trying to be taller than my grandmother, who was also five feet eight. He had a mustache as dark as what hair he had even then. Her hair was fairer, although I never remember anything but the thin white wisps that framed her face as I stood and held her wool. It

95

was remarkable to me that these two were the central figures in one of our all-time favorite family stories: the romance of the century!

I shouldn't have been surprised at my grandfather's determination. He had worked himself through college against great financial odds, except that he was a brilliant man and the college recognized it. And my mother had told me that when she and her two sisters were growing up, my grandfather simply wouldn't discuss any disagreement. What he said was final. Fortunately, my mother had some of that same strong will in her and went right ahead and did what she needed to do.

21 North Pine Avenue:
an address to you,
a history . . . a root . . . to me.
    21 North Pine Avenue:
feet . . . little feet . . . out of the car
  scurrying ahead of our parents
  up the steps . . . across the porch,
a vigorous "Well, let me see you!"
    from our grandfather;
into the house . . . across the hallway.
And where is Grandmother?
In her chair beside the window,
      next to the radio,
  the lamp over her shoulder,
  her lap full of skeins of wool.
The clicking of needles stops . . .
  she peers over her glasses. . . .
A glad and eager "Oh!"
  comes from her mouth
    or is it her heart?
"Oh, you're here!"
Into her arms . . . ensconced by her largeness,
    smothered to her bosom,
  covered with kisses and sighs and exclamations of
    joy.
    21 North Pine Avenue:
    no longer quiet. . . .
Grandchildren mean new life.

Will and Determination

With that same will and determination, David Hutchison arranged to meet Laura Mooney and began to court her. When her father realized that his daughter was interested in this young man who was studying for the Presbyterian ministry, he forbade her to see him.

John Henderson Mooney was the largest wool and leather manufacturer in Canada. The family lived on Sherbrooke Street in Montreal. John Mooney was a successful and prominent businessman who expected his family to accede to his wishes. My grandmother, however, did not want to give up her young man. She asked her mother, Sarah Stewart Mooney, to intercede. (Stewart: there go those clan rights again.) Her mother spoke to her father, but Mr. Mooney said that no daughter of his was going to marry "a poor itinerant preacher"!

Laura was distressed. She had no intention of marrying one of the young men her father found suitable. David called for her again, and this time John Mooney told his daughter that *he* would speak to this Mr. Hutchison. He told my grandfather that marriage was absolutely out of the question, that they couldn't possibly get along on a preacher's wages, that his daughter was used to a way of life that a preacher could not support.

John Mooney was used to being obeyed, but David

Hutchison had a will of iron. He said it was a matter of conscience. He said he loved Laura and would always provide for her, but that he was a man of faith and that Mr. Mooney had no right to interfere with a man's call to the ministry of the Gospel. He said he expected to move to the States and get a pastorate there.

This was even more upsetting to Mr. Mooney. That day he told Laura that he would disinherit her if she insisted on marrying Mr. Hutchison.

Against her father's wishes, Laura Mooney married David Hutchison on June 18, 1895. On June 19 they left for Ottawa. Laura really believed that in time her father would see what a good man her David was and would see how happy she was and would forgive her. She had the assurance from her mother that she would keep trying to help him understand. Unfortunately, Sarah Stewart Mooney died the following August at the age of sixty-three. John Mooney never forgave his daughter.

In my dining room hang beautiful portraits of John and Sarah Mooney. I have the lace collar my great-grandmother is wearing in the portrait. Sometimes I put it around my shoulders and wonder at the sorrow Sarah must have felt to have her daughter and her husband so estranged. Had she lived, would the story have had a different ending?

A postscript to the story is that after a ten-year pastorate in Butte, Montana, my grandfather Hutchison, always a brilliant and studious man, did graduate work at Harvard University and then Harvard Law School, the University of Chicago, the law school at the University of California, and the law school at Union University in Albany. So instead of spending his life as a "poor itinerant preacher," Dr. Hutchison spent his life as an educator, teaching jurisprudence and political science. He was an expert in constitutional law and wrote *The Foundations of the Constitution.* He was often consulted on questions of constitutional and parliamentary law by people from all over the country.

I asked my grandfather once why he was no longer a

minister. He said that he was still a minister and that he took his ordination seriously; he supplied pulpits around the Albany area. But he said he felt he was a better teacher than preacher and he tried to use his Christian faith in the classroom instead of the pulpit.

He was a man of great faith and my grandmother was a woman of great faith, and they knew that they were to pass the faith stories on to their daughters. I've gone through many of the letters from my grandparents to my mother, and each of them always includes a little aid to faith and life. The stories never wear out, but they must be passed on.

It seems that my grandfather had always loved "God's other creatures." He owned two dogs, Rex, a large mongrel with one blue eye and one brown, and Jackie, a onetime hunting dog that went blind. Rex lived to get out, and when he did he terrorized the neighborhood with his wild running about, knocking things and people over. Grandfather would make amends to the neighbors and then come into the house, mildly scolding Rex and then patting him vigorously for fear he'd hurt his feelings.

Jackie had been a good hunting dog, but when we knew her, she spent most of her time bumping into the furniture. She got a lot of sympathy from us and from my grandfather. He used to feed the dogs raw hamburger meat early in the morning while he was cooking his Dr. Jackson's meal. Many a time I watched him put the cereal on the stove, put oatmeal on for Grandmother, go to the refrigerator, take out the package of hamburger meat, and feed bites of it to Rex and to Jackie and have bites of it himself. He told me that he owed his perfect health to raw meat and Dr. Jackson's meal. My mother chastized him once for feeding good meat to the dogs when they could eat dog food. After all, in our household we were in our tuna casserole period and were a bit envious of the dogs! Grandfather replied that God made animals for people to enjoy and that we should be kind to them and treat them well. He had no patience with

100

people who claimed to be Christians and mistreated animals.

Grandfather's devotion to animals carried him to such extremes that each morning, after feeding the dogs, we would go through the ritual of feeding the squirrels and the bluejays. He called them all by name: All the squirrels were named Bobby and all the bluejays were named Jay. He would go to the back door and call out, "Here, Bobby!" and as they came one by one up to the porch, he had a good word for each of them. They would take peanuts out of his hand, and if any of them tried to get more than Grandpa was offering, that particular squirrel would get a lecture on sharing.

When I think of my grandfather calling the squirrels and the jays on that back porch and the squirrels ambling up the cellar door and the jays swirling about his head and the two old dogs close at his heels, it makes me think of St. Francis. My grandfather never wanted to stay on that farm in Orillia, but there was something in him that made him love the animals. In that quiet morning sanctuary, David Hutchison started his day with kindness. When I watch my David throwing crumbs to the birds in the snow or the cold, I think of another time and another David and how God calls us each to our own special expression of faith.

My mother told me that she thought Grandfather left the pastorate because he got too emotionally involved with the lives of the congregation. And he was a good teacher. She said that when I was born, she wrote to him and asked him if he could come to Nashville to baptize me. In a letter written to my mother on September 9, 1934, he said:

About baptizing Ann, I think you had better have Dr. Vance do it. I had such an unfortunate experience regarding the baptism of children when I was in the ministry that I almost came to dislike to baptize a child. They would bring them to me or call me to baptize them when ill and dying. The result was most of the children I baptized died. Of course, not all did that. I know some prominent professional men in Montreal whom I baptized as children. However, so many did die that I came to dislike doing it. I was glad I did not baptize little Charlie. They asked me to do it. Now I think you will understand.

(Little Charlie was my cousin whom I never knew who died after puncturing his stomach and heart climbing on a rusty sled in the summertime.)

There are those
   who don't seem to hear
     the loud *NO*s of life,
   who, no matter what life deals them,
   keep on getting up
     and going on.

Within the family of the faithful,
   I'd venture to say that
   it's not so much a matter of
     strength
   as it is a matter
     of having faith
       in an inner vision—
   in one's God-given dreams.

To Give
and to Receive

I take my cup of tea into the living room and wonder about these families in which God chooses to place us. It is in the family that we learn to give and to receive. It is in the family that we learn to be other-centered rather than self-centered. It is in the family that we learn to touch the untouchables of this world because God asks that of us. Love the unlovables. Unstranger the strangers. Reach out to the unreachable. It is in the family that we learn whether we are to live in faith and promise or to live for security. It is in the family that we learn to yearn . . . for faithfulness.

My mother had parents who lived their faith daily; my father had parents who lived their faith daily. Both sets of parents lived their faith and told the stories of faith to their children. It is not surprising that my mother and my father found each other—even in New York City in the 1920s. They met in church!

My father was student assistant at the First Presbyterian Church on Fifth Avenue. My mother had set up her law practice there and had promised her mother that she would go to church in the Big City. My mother and father met at a young adult group for which he had responsibility.

They were married on October 28, 1927, in Gladys's home in Albany. They wanted to be married in the church and I was surprised they weren't. However, my grandfather said that if they were married in the church, "they would have to invite a big crowd to the reception and it would be too expensive." So they married at home.

My father soon had a call to a church in Nashville as the assistant to the very distinguished pastor, Dr. James I. Vance. At the age of thirty-six he succeeded Dr. Vance (who had retired because of ill health) as the minister of this large and influential congregation.

I remember the First Presbyterian Church in Nashville with a great deal of fondness. I used to go with my father to church early on Sunday morning. My mother would bring the other three children later. I loved going early so that I could wander around that big old church by myself. My favorite thing (besides riding the elevator up and down) was going into the fellowship hall and clicking around that brown linoleum floor with my patent leather shoes. I could make all the noise I wanted to.

One Sunday morning I wandered into the sanctuary. I couldn't have been more than five or six, but I remember it so vividly. For the first time I got a really good look at that sanctuary. It looked like the inside of an Egyptian temple. I suppose that I had learned something about the Christian faith because I was suddenly offended by that sanctuary. My father came in shortly thereafter to do whatever it is ministers do on Sunday morning in the sanctuary, and I asked him why our church had to look like an Egyptian temple. He said that he and my mother had asked themselves the same question when they first came to Nashville, but he said they had come to love it. It can remind the people of their Old Testament roots:

> Once we were slaves and now we are free;
> Once we were no people and now we are God's people.

And he said the people of God must be about their business of ending slavery and creating anew.

I was just a child, and during church services I used to sit and count the lights and the decorations on the Egyptian columns and wish the service were over, but somewhere along the way I discovered that I was one of God's people and that God's people had to be about their business of ending slavery and creating anew.

My father is a man of conscience who was concerned with the slavery in this world, whether racial or economic or political. As assistant pastor, my father had already aligned himself with an organization known as the Tennessee Inter-racial Association and he had spoken out in favor of higher wages for industrial workers. He had gotten some flack about these issues, but since Dr. Vance was senior minister, no one seemed unduly alarmed. My father asked James Weldon Johnson to come and speak, and as he read parts of *God's Trombones,* many in the congregation wept.

His call was not unanimous, and Grandfather Hutchison warned him that those in the minority would cause trouble later. They did.

In the South my father preached a sermon on racial brotherhood. Some of the session members came to him and asked him to stick to the Bible in his preaching. He said he was preaching the Christian message found in the Bible, that all people should "Love one another."

During the period between the two world wars, everybody was for peace. My father preached a sermon at Southwestern at Memphis (that both Todd and I attended). His topic was "Ain't Gonna Study War No More." My father felt the rising temperature of those who called for war, and as a Christian he felt it his responsibility to preach the gospel of the Prince of Peace. It was a word he had heard for years. As Christians we live for others. If we're fighting and killing others, are we following the Prince of Peace?

One of the songs during World War II was "Praise the Lord and Pass the Ammunition." It was a catchy tune, and one evening at supper my parents told us they hoped we wouldn't sing that song because they found it irreverent. You could either praise the Lord or pass the ammunition. We didn't sing it.

One Sunday morning my father felt that it was his responsibility to lead the congregation in seeking after peace. He preached a sermon on peace. In today's church atmosphere of preaching peace, it wouldn't raise an eyebrow. In those prewar days it was dynamite. He was preaching his conscience just as those before him had done, from the Scots who crossed the water to his mother raising a family by herself.

Immediately after the service a session meeting was held and a resolution was adopted ordering my father not to preach on war.

At the regular session meeting my father said, "With reference to the resolution passed by the session on my sermon dealing with the possibility of war, I want to say that if this was brotherly advice, I will receive it with gratitude. If it was to instruct me on what to preach, I cannot accept it, for only God can tell me what to preach."

Eventually both the Session and the Board of Deacons felt my father should resign. In a newspaper interview (and it was front-page news) my father said, "It is not whether I remain or leave, but whether or not a minority group in a church is to be allowed to precipitate such a situation and then clamor that because of the resulting dissension their purposes must be served and the will of the majority thwarted." In a congregational vote the majority expressed a vote of confidence in my father.

The Presbytery's Commission on the Minister and His Work (of which my father was chairman) felt that for the "good of all" my father should leave. He told them that it was a matter of conscience and it was their responsibility to come to a decision. Their decision was that he should resign.

From the minutes of the Nashville Presbytery:

The Commission records its very high regard for Rev. Thos. C. Barr, and its confidence that in his ministry with this church, including the period of recent development of disunity, he has acted in sincerity, with an earnest purpose to be faithful to his high calling as a minister of Christ, to be fearless in proclaiming the truth which his Master would have him proclaim, that he has sought to follow Christ in the spirit in which he has dealt with officers and members of the congregation and with all men in relationships. However, the Commission believes that the present state of disunity in the church and the measure of opposition to his continuing as its pastor is such as to preclude hope for a united church under his leadership, and therefore declares the pastoral relationship dissolved, effective as of September 14th, 1942.

My father, moderator of the presbytery at the time, appealed to the next judicatory, the Synod, saying that the Commission had no authority to dissolve the relationship.

The Synod upheld my father, saying that the Presbytery Commission had no authority to act. When he felt he was vindicated, my father resigned. His conscience wouldn't let him preach in a pulpit that was not free. Like the Scots who went before him, he would not worship by someone else's dictates.

There were others in the church who would not be dictated to. Over a number of months they had formed a committee, and they wanted to start a new church with my father as its leader. At first he was reluctant because he did not want to be responsible for a split. They told him they were going to start this new church whether he came or not.

My father did not want to be disruptive. He wanted to be as faithful to his calling as possible. He finally decided to go with them, and those years were happy, faithful ones—for him, for the church, and for us as a family. I was one of the first charter members of the church.

I was only eight years old when I became a charter member, but I had listened to my parents as they talked about what they ought to do. I had been through the pros and the cons. I had listened to the prayers and the pleas. I had seen my father agonize for fear he was not being faithful to the God who had sent him to minister. I had seen my mother hold her head high and support my father when so many were criticizing him. I had seen the many friends flock to him and tell him he was doing the right thing. My brother and I sat at the top of the stairs when we were supposed to be in bed and listened to the new church members work out their path. I had seen a new light in my father's eyes, and somehow in my eight-year-old heart I understood what it meant to stand up for what you think is right, what it meant to be Christian in fact and not name only, for my father had taken that risk and now, instead of being the minister of a socially prominent, large church with a decent salary, he was the minister of a struggling little church that couldn't afford to pay its minister a whole lot, but he had his integrity and we all had our faith and its promises.

Who are your people? My father was a wandering South Carolinian who preached racial brotherhood and peace in a South that was not ready to hear that word. He was called "nigger lover" and "Communist" by other church people. Many a person would have crumbled under that load, many a person could have rationalized that the timing was wrong, that it was possible to work within the system. My father could not. He is a humble man; he did not preach in arrogance or belligerence. He gently told the Good News, but it was bad news to many who heard it.

He spoke out
     when others would have kept quiet.
He stood up
     when others would have run.
He risked and lost
          position
          monetary gain
          prestige
     when others would have rationalized.
It was not that he was courageous—
    He was faithful.

Kneeling
in Bethlehem

The organizing church had 245 members when it came into being on November 1, 1942. We met first in the old Corinthian Lodge on West End Avenue. Then Trinity Presbyterian Church bought property on Hillsboro Road, a twenty-five-acre estate with a marvelous English Tudor-style house. It was huge and we loved it.

I really don't know how my mother put up with all the Sunday morning rush. She had to see to it that four children were bathed and fed and dressed and that the downstairs was cleaned before eight thirty in the morning. We finally got a door that locked for the head of the stairs because so many of the congregation would wander upstairs while we were desperately trying to get ready. But manage it she did.

They were wonderful days, really. I remember church picnics out back where the kids could have as much soda as they wanted. The men would put it in big wooden tubs of ice. I drank twelve large grape sodas throughout one hot summer's day. Well, it was beastly hot waiting in line to ride the ponies.

And the church pageants! I longed to be an angel. I knew right from the beginning I couldn't be a king. My brother was going to be a king one year when we were still meeting down at the Corinthian Lodge. He would practice at home, walking around in a kingly fashion, chin up, gift in hand. I asked my mother why I couldn't be a king. She was sensitive enough to say that maybe someday I could be when I was a little older. But my brother said I could never be a king —not because I was a girl but because I didn't know what frankincense was! He was right, but then he was always right.

I was thrilled when the choices for the pageant participants were announced one year. As I said, I was dying to be an angel. By the time I was an angel, I wanted to be Mary. And since I was the minister's daughter, I was Mary—when I was sixteen years old.

I can remember it just like it was yesterday. The church was on a hill surrounded by acres of land and looked out over Hillsboro Road, which was actually a highway. Each night the week before Christmas we would put on the pageant and many cars would pull over to watch and to listen, for we had a loudspeaker that carried the Scripture and the music out into the night. It was a very professional endeavor, for Bob Quinn, who was with a radio station, directed us. We had a life-size realistic-looking stable, complete with real cows and donkeys and sheep. The choir was magnificent. Bob read the Scripture and he had a voice like an archangel. And I was Mary.

I remember exactly what I wore: an azure blue robe and a lighter blue scarf around my head and makeup! I was Mary! I was holy! I felt absolutely ethereal.

Joseph came with his donkey to pick me up at the house beyond the church. We started down the driveway and then at a certain point came across the grass, making our way in the heavenly night to Bethlehem. It was my moment. I was entranced by the holiness of it all. All eyes were on me!

I had not, however, counted on the performance of my little brother, Bill. He was an angel. That was not typecasting. Bill is the child my mother had tested for deafness because he talked so loudly. He is also the child she dragged to school when he was five and insisted that the principal keep him there all day. She didn't care about the rules; she was desperate!

While I was preoccupied with my role as Mary, Bill was

practicing his angel techniques. He had a mark in the stable where he was to kneel, and he had practiced it and practiced it. He knew his kneeling place.

When Mary and Joseph came around closer to the stable, when I was at my most ethereal, I got a glimpse of my little brother. His once-white angel gown was splattered with mud and his big brown oxfords that had kicked me under the table many a time were thick with it. His halo was definitely at a rakish angle and he stood there in some sort of halfway annunciating position that left a lot to be desired. He caught my eye and put his hands to his ears and stuck out his tongue at me.

I was furious. Zoom! I came right down off that mountaintop. Then I watched as he angelically elbowed a couple of shepherds on either side who had dared to come close to his kneeling spot. Shepherds dominoed, but there was Bill, hands under his chin, angelically kneeling in Bethlehem. Mary was not pleased.

After the pageant I ran, disgraced, up to the house and asked my mother how she could have had such a child. She answered that she barely noticed it and that people always thought the children were cute and after all, he had found his kneeling place in Bethlehem.

Yes, it was Bill, not I, who knew what it was like to yearn after that kneeling place in Bethlehem. I just wanted to be holier than thou. I wanted everybody to think I was beautiful and saintly.

Who are my people? They are those who yearn to kneel in Bethlehem . . . faithful to the Christ-child who waits even now for us to come.

Mary,
    Nazareth girl:
What did you know of ethereal beings
    with messages from God?
What did you know of men
    when you found yourself with child?
What did you know of babies,
    you, barely out of childhood yourself?
God-chosen girl:
What did you know of God
    that brought you to this stable
        blessed among women?
Could it be that you had been ready
                    waiting
                    listening
                      for the footsteps
    of an angel?
Could it be there are messages for us
    if we have the faith to listen?

Christmas in a World at War

During the years of World War II my mother, who had a law degree, worked as a substitute teacher so her hours could be the same as ours at school. Then later she worked at the Vultee plant as a supervisor.

My father had volunteered to be a chaplain, but he was not called. He was torn by his feeling that he was needed as a chaplain and his feeling that he was needed here among those who were left.

I remember the day that a dear woman who was my seventh-grade teacher heard the news that her son had been killed in action. My father went to be with her. When she heard, she fell and broke her leg. There were others, too many. My secret fear was that our father would go and never come back.

We made our way through those days, doing what we could. We had a victory garden and we took the top and bottom off the tin cans and stamped on them with our feet to flatten them so that the metal could be used again. And we prayed that the war would be over, that the killing would cease, that the families would be reunited. My father got extra gas ration stamps because he was a minister and needed them to call on the sick and bereaved, but he tried to curtail their use because he didn't want to take advantage. The Sunday afternoon driving ceased.

A high point in the day was waiting for our father to come

home. Late in the afternoons we used to meet him at the bottom of the long driveway so that we could jump onto the running boards and ride up to the house.

When the war was over and finances were a little better, my mother began to write. She wrote short stories and then serials for church papers and magazines and then she wrote historical fiction. She wrote about Martin Luther and John Knox and John Calvin and the Children's Crusades and John Bunyan.

In spite of her many and varied interests my mother always had time for us. She felt a responsibility to pass her faith along to us. She was always there for us. My friends adored her. She was always in the thick of things: giving us ghost parties where the table would rise in the dark, letting my brother have a spook house every Halloween, letting him bring snakes into the house, letting me bring stray cats and dogs home, letting my sister take harp lessons (harp lessons!), letting my little brother be my energetic full-of-himself little brother, allowed to play football when it scared her to death.

I used to love the way she decorated the Christmas tree. We would all be in the living room, getting out the various decorations, placing them on the tree, and she would be in the kitchen cooking up a storm. We all wanted her to come be with us, so she would run back and forth, stirring something and then return to grab a handful of tinsel and throw it haphazardly on the tree. Oh, what Christmases we had!

The Session had a habit of giving my father one hundred new one-dollar bills on Christmas Eve afternoon. We knew we didn't have a lot to spend on Christmas even though it seemed glorious to us. We would wait patiently and quietly until the gift was delivered and then, as soon as the Elder would leave, we would jump up and down and scream with happiness. Each of us would get a certain amount of money and all six of us would pile into the car and go to the five-and-ten-cent store to do our last-minute Christmas shopping. A lot of things had been reduced by that time, and we thought the five-and-ten-cent store was the perfect place to shop. We would divide up and then try to keep the other five from seeing us as we made our purchases. I know my mother got far too many bottles of Evening in Paris!

One year I wanted a suede jacket for Christmas. I wanted it badly, but my mother said we couldn't afford it and I understood that. My father and mother always made a point of doing something for somebody else and made us a part of that. I went into many a home that was cold and cheerless, taking food my mother had cooked and toys we no longer used or toys that had been purchased so that these families could have some sort of a Christmas. We saw firsthand how some people in this world had to live, and it was made very clear to us that we were wealthy compared to most of the world's people. We knew that as Christians we were to share what we had.

So I didn't expect a suede jacket. We opened the presents and were cleaning up afterward, throwing papers into the fireplace, which had not been lighted since it was so warm out that year. There in the fireplace was a large box with a tag that read: "Ann, aren't you going to open me?" It was my suede jacket. I knew that someone had sacrificed so that I could have it. It was a gift of love!

Who are your people? My mother was a wandering New Yorker who dwelt in the land of the sun with my father and her children, giving us her faith.

It was a family treasure,
      that vase,
         that golden vase,
      the vase that had belonged to my
            great-grandmother,
      to my grandmother, and now to my mother. . . .
And the vase sat on the mantel
      out of reach of little fingers.
However, I managed to reach it;
         I climbed to reach it;
         I broke it,
         the family treasure.
Golden pieces of once a family treasure
      valueless
      that moments before was priceless.
And I began to cry,
      then louder, in sobs that brought
         my mother running.
I could hardly get it out:
      "I broke the vase . . . the treasure."
And then my mother gave to me a gift:
      A look of relief over her face and
      "Oh, I thought you'd been hurt!"
And then she hugged to her the one who had
      just moments before
         broken the family treasure.
She gave to me a gift:
      She made it very clear that
      I was the family treasure.
      I was what was priceless
         and of great value.
She also made it very clear
      where her heart was.

From the 1982–83 Stewardship Theme Materials, *Multiply the Gift* by Ann Weems, Presbyterian Church (U.S.A.). Used by permission. Related Scripture: Matt. 6:19–21.

I Hope You Get
Your Feelings Hurt

Mother, now I am Mother and the responsibility is passed on to me. From mother to mother to mother . . . from father to father to father. "May the words of my mouth and the meditations of my heart be acceptable to Thee" and may these, your children, have the eyes to see and the ears to hear.

I move from my chair to the window and look out. I see Heather making her way across the snowy street. I am always astonished to see how beautiful she is, this daughter of mine. Beautiful to look at . . . even more beautiful to know. Her heart is tender and kind and she enriches my every day. How can I be sure that my words and my meditations are acceptable? Is the responsibility too large for our human frailty? In my heart I hug her to me. When she gets to the door, I hug her to me physically and she smiles. "Hi, Mom. How was your day?"

"Good," I answer. "You know how much your mother loves the snow."

"You made a fire."

"Yes."

She looks at me. Does she know, does she remember that Todd made the fires? Slowly, she says, "The saddest thing happened today. You know the boy I was telling you about with the sister who was dying?" I nod. "Well, she died. He wasn't at school. I think when he comes back, I'll say something to him, but I don't know what to say."

Oh, darling, the words of your mother and the meditations of your heart will be acceptable to God—and to that boy.

Five years old, sitting at the kitchen table,
          elbows table-edge,
                chin in hands,
                      tears glistening in those dark eyes.
"You want to tell me about it?" I ventured.
Small voice: "I got my feelings hurt."
"Did somebody say something to you?"
Louder now: "Yes . . . the teacher said that some children
     have big tummies swollen sick because they don't have
     enough to eat."
Tears rolling down the face now: "When I grow up I'm
     going to give all my money to the children who don't
     have enough to eat, because when they don't have
     enough to eat, I get my feelings hurt."
O God in Heaven, hear your child.
Five years old. . . . How did he know what some of us never
     learn?
That it's only when our feelings are hurt that we will do
     something.
When our feelings are hurt . . . when we feel the hurt . . .
     we are willing to do something
          like live out our faith
               in the hope of a day when all the children of the earth
               will be fed.
I hope you get your feelings hurt. . . .

Snow and Hot Chocolate

I look back out the window. "I didn't know it was snowing again." Heather joins me.

"Have you been thinking about your grandmother again?"

I laugh. "My grandmother and all the rest. Does it show?"

She laughs. "A little. Want me to make you a cup of hot chocolate?"

Of course.

I love hot chocolate! Snow and hot chocolate. I remember a time when I drank cup after cup. The snow of 1951 in Nashville. What a storm that was!

Our mother was in Albany visiting her father. Grandmother had died in 1949. Now Mother was due back on the train that very day. We all bundled up and with our father walked to the Union Station through the deep snow right down the middle of the street all the way to town except for an occasional run to the side of the road for an occasional car. Most cars wouldn't start or their owners were safely at home. School was called off; work was called off. Life was interrupted for over a week. It was wonderful! At least it was wonderful for somebody who wanted to go sledding and drink hot chocolate. It wasn't so wonderful that the water pipes burst. It wasn't so wonderful that we didn't have any heat. We slept by the fireplace and went down to the church to wash up.

For energy we ate chocolate bars on the way to the station. Of course the train wasn't on time. We were waiting sleepily at midnight with still no word about when the train would make it through. We had talked to my grandfather and he had put her on the train. So she was somewhere between Albany and Nashville. My little brother was asleep. Jane and I were nodding. A friend of my father's was there, and he agreed to take us back to the church. He had a car that worked and had chains. We slept that night in the kitchen of the church, warmed by the open oven.

The next day my mother arrived and in no time had everything under control: hot soup on the stove, plans for making snow ice cream, advice for getting our clothing dry after we'd been out sledding. She turned it all into a party. My father was busy trying to see that people in the city were warm and well fed, but he would put in some sledding time too, as well as time in keeping the logs coming up those stairs to the bedrooms.

Once we had a snow here in St. Louis and I was afraid to drive to the grocery. Todd came home and said he'd be happy to go to McDonald's. He did and returned safely and gave me my change. I discovered it was five dollars too much. Todd was stricken. He had not counted it. He got back in the car, drove through the snow, and returned the five dollars to the boy who had waited on him. When he got home he explained that it would have come out of the boy's salary that night. The boy was shocked that Todd had returned the money.

Stuart and a couple of his friends spent all afternoon one day after school getting people out of the ruts they were stuck in out in front of our house. He came in saying, "You know some of those people wanted to pay us? Why would we take any money? We were just helping them out!"

There's something about a snowstorm that makes people convivial, something that makes them act like family. A few years back, in a particularly bad snowstorm which stopped the city of St. Louis for several days, people were going out of their way to be helpful to others. They were taking food to people unable to get their own. They were taking blankets and kerosene heaters to the ones whose power was cut off or were too poor to have heat. They were shoveling snow for the neighbor who had no one to help. David was a deacon to a woman who lived by herself. He went to check on her to be sure she was all right. What he did for her was to talk to her. She was terribly lonely.

People were doing things off the top of their hearts, without thinking about them. That's the way families act, and when you get right down to it, we're all descended from the same family. My mother would say, If that's true, then Adam must have been a Stuart!

Families that are families do do things off the top of their hearts. They love fiercely because they have first been loved. When you've been loved, you can love, and we've all been loved by the God of love who gave us what was most precious to him, his Son. If we as humans can feel such extravagant love for our children, think how God must love us!

My sister, Jane, has always been one to do things off the top of her heart. When she was in college she worked very hard to win a collection of the complete works of Shakespeare. When she did win, she gave her prize to me! She is still giving to me with little thought for the cost to her. Off the top of her heart!

God's love is not a controlling love. We are sent out to be faithful, but we aren't awakened each morning with a list of things to do that day in order to be faithful.

I know that we as parents are sometimes controlling. When our boys were little, I was visiting Gladys and Daddy in Nashville in that wonderful big manse. It was June and hot, and flies and mosquitoes were rampant and three little boys ran in and out of the house slamming that screen door in the living room that led to the porch. Gladys and I were talking and she had made lemonade and the pitcher was sitting on the coffee table and we kept being interrupted by small boys appearing and disappearing. I spoke to them, but it didn't seem to register. The television had been snapped on during one of these entrances, and left on even though no one was watching it. A noted child psychiatrist came on, and my mother and I stopped talking to listen to him. "If," he said, "you want your child to stop doing something that you don't like, you say to him, calmly: 'That wasn't very helpful, was it?'"

Just at that moment, Todd burst into the room, slammed the screen door, slid on the Oriental rug, lost his balance, and knocked the pitcher of lemonade, glasses, and ice onto the rug.

In my calmest voice I said, "Todd, that wasn't very helpful, was it?"

He looked at me innocently and answered, "I wasn't meaning to be helpful." So much for that child psychiatrist!

In the light of raw honesty, one can see clearer. The boys were coming in and out of the door because they wanted to check on us, they wanted to be with us, and yet wanted to run free. Isn't that what we all want to do? We need each other, and yet we want the freedom to do what we think is right. Isn't that the way God works? God is there for us when we call, but God allows us the freedom to make decisions. Of course, we have guidance. We're not just doing our own thing. The guidance is in a Book we far too often talk about instead of read!

When Heather was about eight or nine, she came into the house and told me that she had just been quizzed by a group of people who said they were Bible people. She said that one of the women seemed irritated when she didn't know who one of the biblical characters was. They told Heather she should go to their church. Heather was mad, but she was also embarrassed that she didn't know the answers. I told her that she could always learn the answers, but that she already had the spirit of the message of the Bible, which they appeared to have completely overlooked in their evangelistic fervor.

Martin Marty spoke at an Adult Education Series at the church we were in in Monmouth, Illinois, years ago—twenty-seven years ago, to be exact. I wanted to hear him, but Stuart was a baby and I either couldn't afford or couldn't find a sitter. I decided to take him and sit in the balcony in case he got fussy. Just as Dr. Marty was finishing his lecture and just as he made a very important point, Stuart cried out, "Hsilentilsotnneihfgonjur," or whatever babies say. Dr. Marty said, "I couldn't have said it better myself."

A sense of humor is so important while we're telling our faith stories. When we get so caught up in our own drivenness in telling the Good News that we think we're the only ones who know the Good News, we're in trouble. When we make a little child feel bad because she doesn't know all the names of the biblical characters, we're not telling good news. When we tell a child that one church has *the* truth, we're not telling good news.

The story that we tell doesn't come from one church; it comes from the heart of God. After you've read my family stories, you know just how Presbyterian I am. In fact when Stuart was five years old and learning to read, he would read various signs as we drove along the road: Coca-Cola . . . STOP, etc. Then one day he said, "Oh, look, Mommy, PRESBYTERIAN CROSSING!"

Yes, we're Presbyterian, and my father and I are mighty glad to be back in the same church, but the bottom line is not Presbyterianism; the bottom line is the faith story of our Lord Jesus Christ. We who have lived out our lives in the church are in danger of substituting the story of the church for the story of the gospel. Just because we hang around the building a lot doesn't mean we're doing the work of the Lord!

Sarah,
    you are not the only one to laugh at God,
      nor are you the only one to deny it.
We who claim to be the faithful
    laugh at God's promises.
Oh, we deny it on Sunday morning,
    but go out laughing on Monday.
If we really believed God
    we wouldn't be bowing down to security at any
      expense.
Old as we are,
    if we really believed,
    we'd be out giving birth
      to a world where we all loved each other
      even as much as we love ourselves.

The Methodist Connection

Don's family has a Methodist background. When his mother died, I met a man whose story I had heard many times, but he told it from his point of view, which gave me a new insight into the faith of my in-laws. When the man was quite young, he fell in with a group that was wild. He began drinking and found that he couldn't stop it even when his young wife threatened to leave him. Finally, the jolt of her departure made him take a look at his life. He had lost his wife and his money and his job. He needed to get back on his feet. He applied to my father-in-law for a job as a dishwasher in his restaurant. He talked to both Don's mother and father, and they asked him a lot of questions about his background. He told them all about himself, but he said he was determined to change. They gave him the job and warned him that he could not drink. He asked for an advance on his salary so he could get a place to live and they told him he didn't have enough money for a decent place and then they offered to let him live in the empty bedroom in their house. Soon he was on the way to recovery and he began going to the Methodist church with them. After a while he enrolled in college. When he graduated he told them he wanted to go to seminary. He told me that he could never have been successful if it had not been for the Weemses, who took him in when they didn't know him and had enough faith in him to see him through. He is now a bishop in the Methodist Church. He told me that through the years he tells his story wherever he goes as an encouragement to other people who feel they have nothing. The Weemses trusted him when he was not a person to inspire trust. They took in a stranger and fed and clothed him and introduced him to a faith that gave him life. He, in turn, has spent his life passing on this faith.

When Heather was three, she was enrolled in a preschool sponsored by the high school for students interested in child care. The children ranged in age from six months to five years. One of the children was a newly adopted three-year-old Vietnamese child whose father was on the faculty at Washington University and whose mother was from India. The little boy knew no English and had not learned any in the two months he had been in St. Louis. The teachers and the mother told me that the little boy didn't want to be left at school, but Heather took him by the hand and took him over to the sand table where there were toys. Later, when they were to go out to play, they were to climb through the window and play in the yard beside the school. He was afraid to do that, but Heather took him by the hand and he went and had a great time. He became her shadow and she explained to him patiently and lovingly all the things they were to do. He sat next to her at the table; he sat next to her on the rug for story time; he followed her to the gym, where he whizzed around in the little cars and on the tricyle, laughing with Heather all the time. At home and at school the parents and teachers would repeat words for him to say, but he did not speak in English. Heather continued to talk to him constantly, explaining everything to him, but she never asked him to repeat what she had said. They got along just great. One day the mother greeted me enthusiastically and exclaimed that the little boy had said his first word in English. The word was Heather!

Gradually, the child began to chat with Heather and then, of course, with everybody. The teachers and the mother said that Heather had used all the right means of education. Fortunately, they had seen what was taking place and knew that, with patience, the little boy would learn in an easy, natural way.

There are times in our faith journeys when we cannot speak the language, when we feel we are in a foreign land, when we are afraid and don't want to be pushed; nor do we want to repeat what someone else is asking us to mimic. With patience and with loving-kindness, we are enabled to hear the faith stories, we are enabled to see the faith shining in somebody else, and we find that we too can speak because somebody took the time to hold out a hand to us.

There is a cry in mainline Protestantism for effective evangelism. There is no more effective evangelism than telling our stories to those we care about: to family, to friends, to those we see day in and day out. Few of us came to Christianity by a blinding experience. Most of us are in the church because our faith was passed on to us by parents and family or by friends in the church family, and it happened to us over a number of years, not a number of minutes.

Don has built his ministry on this patient, loving style of evangelism. He does not push people to join the church. He preaches the Christian faith in an inclusive, vital way, making it very clear that it is within the church a person can find family . . . can find life. Jesus said he came that we might have life, and have it abundantly. Within the church, no matter the denomination, we share our faith stories by patiently living our faith, by loving mercy, by doing justice, and by living humbly because we know that all of life comes from God. We evangelize by telling the Good News to our children, to our friends, to the world in which we live; we evangelize by the way in which we live out our faith stories.

Last Sunday Don preached about faith. He told the story of Zacchaeus and pointed out the humor in the story: Here's a funny little man climbing a tree to get a glimpse of Jesus. He didn't care if people ridiculed him; he was determined to see Jesus. Often we care very much about what people think because we take ourselves so seriously. Perhaps if we took ourselves less seriously and our faith more seriously, the world could see Jesus more clearly.

Years ago my father preached a sermon whose theme I've never forgotten. He said that we are who we are at home. It's not too hard to be pleasant and polite and kind to the world, but home, where we let our hair down, is where we really are who we are. It is there that our children are hearing our faith stories . . . or not hearing them.

And in the church we are who we are at congregational meetings, or in the church dining room, or on the boards, or at the women's meetings, or in church school. The way in which we live out our faith becomes our faith story to the world. When the stories are that we are feeding the hungry or visiting the imprisoned or comforting the sick or fighting racial prejudice or working against an oppressive economic order that works against the poor, when we are patiently holding out our hand to a world that cannot speak, when we are about our business of freeing slaves, we are telling faith stories. When our church looks with compassion upon the world, the world will have the eyes to see who our Lord is.

Into the wild and painful cold of the starless winter night
    came the refugees,
Slowly making their way to the border.
The man, stooped from age or anxiety,
    hurried his small family through the wind.
Bearded and dark, his skin rough and cracked from the
        cold,
    his frame looming large in spite of the slumped
        shoulders:
He looked like a man who could take care of whatever
        came at them
    from the dark.
Unless, of course, there were too many of them.
One man he could handle . . . two, even . . . , but a
        border patrol . . .
    they wouldn't have a chance.
His eyes, black and alert,
    darted from side to side, then over his shoulder,
        then back again forward.
Had they been seen?
Had they been heard?
Every rustle of wind, every sigh from the child,
    sent terror through his chest.
Was this the way?
Even the stars had been unkind—
    had hidden themselves in the ink of night
        so that the man could not read their way.
Only the wind . . . was it enough?
Only the wind and his innate sense of direction. . . .
What kind of a cruel judgment would that be,
    to wander in circles through the night?
Or to safely make their way to the border
    only to find the authorities waiting for them?
He glanced at the young woman, his young bride.

132

No more than a child herself,
    she nuzzled their newborn, kissing his neck.
She looked up, caught his eye, and smiled.
Oh, how the homelessness had taken its toll on her!
Her eyes were red, her young face lined,
    her lovely hair matted from inattention,
        her clothes stained from milk and baby,
            her hands chapped from the raw wind of winter.
She'd hardly had time to recover from childbirth
    when word had come that they were hunted,
        and they fled with only a little bread, the
            remaining wine,
        and a very small portion of cheese.
Suddenly, the child began to make small noises.
The man drew his breath in sharply;
    the woman quietly put the child to breast.
Fear . . . long dread-filled moments. . . .
Huddled, the family stood still in the long silence.
At last the man breathed deeply again,
    reassured they had not been heard.
And into the night continued
    Mary and Joseph and the Babe.

His Name
Is Immanuel

"You know what is good . . . to do justice, to love mercy, to walk humbly with your God." I say that over and over to myself. It's so easy to be pious on our way to Bethlehem.

Don told me that he's been humbled several times, but two of his favorites concern our son David and our grandson Barrett. When we were leaving the Webster Groves Church, where Don was associate with George Sweazey, there was a farewell service in the sanctuary. I had taken the boys with me and was sitting in the back in case I needed to get out with them. David was three and he couldn't see over all the people in front of us, but he could hear the voices. The Call to Worship was given by Dr. Chester Carnahan, another associate at the church. He had a deep voice, and after he'd spoken, David asked, "Who was that? God?"

The next voice was that of his father, and I thought he would recognize him, but he asked, "Who was that? Charlie Brown?"

Last Christmas, when Barrett was visiting us, we went to the Christmas Eve service. Since it didn't begin until eleven and since it was six below zero that night, we bundled Barrett up in his pajamas and set out for church. He was between Stuart and me, and when he saw Don coming down the aisle in his robe and Advent stole, he said, "Look, there's Grandpa in his bathrobe with a towel around his neck." He obviously thought the attire was informal!

Humility . . . My mother used to recite, "The greatest among you shall be the servant of all." She told me once that she thought the best way to raise children was to behave the way you wanted them to behave. They would learn by following.

Of course, that's easier said than done, but in the church family, children have many adults to follow, and the faith stories multiply. Of course we make mistakes on this faith journey. Of course we make poor choices. Of course we are often faithless. Part of the story is that of a forgiving God. God is not only faithful, God through Jesus Christ is faithful on our behalf. The good news is that God is with us. *And you "shall call his name Immanuel."*

When I was a small child, a woman in the church named Miss Hester used to baby-sit for us. We called her Nee Nee; I don't remember why. Nee Nee was at our house quite often through the years, and when we got old enough to no longer need a baby-sitter, Nee Nee would still come from time to time because we had become her family. As years went by, Nee Nee got forgetful. She spent the night with us one Christmas Eve. She was sleeping in the room with me in one of the twin beds, and when she woke up, she said, "Where am I?" I got up right away and said, "Nee Nee, it's all right. It's Ann. You're at our house. It's Christmas morning." She had a bewildered look on her face, the look of a lost child. I felt as though through the years we had exchanged places. She had gone from caretaker to being the one in need of care, and I had gone from one needing care to caretaker. She looked up at me and said, "Well, I don't know where I am, but the good news is you're with me."

The good news is God is with us. God has called us together in a faith family. God has given us faith stories to help us live out our faith.

Heather said to me one day, "Just think, Mom, these are my good old days."

I've thought a lot about the good old days. I'm grateful for them, but we've all got to live in the good new days. We've got a lot of living to do in the present.

Who are my people? My people are those who dream dreams, for our God is a God who keeps promises, and in this life, even in the darkness, God gives us Light; even in suffering God gives us hope, even in our faithlessness, God is faithful. Even when we think we are useless, there are birds to feed or hands to hold. Even when our places of worship are taken from us, there is a tree under which we may pray.

In the church even those who have no family have a family, for Christ has called us all into his family and has asked us to be faithful.

One Sunday morning when Heather was a baby, she woke up with a cold and a little fever. I asked Stuart if he would stay with her while I went to church. He said he just had to go to church; they were in the middle of a great discussion in the senior high class. I asked Todd if he would take care of Heather. He said he had a deacons' meeting and didn't want to miss Dad's sermon. I thought good old David would come through for me, but he said not today. In his church school class they were working on a newspaper for the congregation. I finally had to get a neighbor. Later I said to Don, "What is this world coming to when the minister's children don't want to miss church?"

The truth of the matter is we all want to go to church. It's at church where the faith family can have their family reunion every Sunday. It's there we can tell our family faith stories and help each other to live them. It's there that our successes can be applauded and our failures understood. It's there that we can begin to understand the good news.

The good news is that in spite of our faithlessness, God has given us Immanuel. Sometimes we may not know where we are, but the good news is that God is with us.

Heather returns with the hot chocolate and joins me by the fire. David will soon be home, and then Don. Maybe we'll call Stuart tonight. I heard Minneapolis had twelve inches. I turn to Heather. "So these are your good old days?"

She smiles and looks through some family pictures. "Who are these people?" she asks.

"Oh, just some wandering Arameans."

What concerns me,
　　what lies on my heart
　　　is this:
That we in the church
　　　　　　papered and programmed
　　　　　　articulate and agenda-ed
　　are telling the faith story
　　　　　　　all wrong,
　　are telling it as though it happened two thousand
　　　　years ago
　　　or is going to happen
　　as soon as the church budget is raised.
We seem to forget that Christ's name is Immanuel,
　　　God With Us,
Not just when he sat among us
　　　　　　but *now*,
　　when we cannot feel the nailprints in his hands.

The Family of Faith

My family faith stories are not extraordinary. They could be stories of any number of families. The important thing is that every generation has taught its children that our roots are roots of faith.

When I was a child, we used to beg our parents to do something by saying, "Everybody's doing it!" We soon learned that we weren't Everybody. We were those who were committed to a faith that expressed love and justice for the nobodies of this world as well as for the Somebodies and even for the Everybodys.

My inheritance has been this faith, but my responsibility is to leave it to the next generation.

In the church we are all in a faith family, and we have our faith stories written in the pages of the Book. Our faith is our inheritance, and we have the responsibility to tell our faith stories so that others can hear them.

Each Palm Sunday our congregation meets in the room beneath the sanctuary to go in procession with our palms, out the side door and around to the front door into the sanctuary. We are led by bagpipers who play their hearts out. One year, Dr. Walter Brueggemann was preaching, and he and Don and the bagpipers were leading the happy procession when a young man in the apartment house across the street threw up the window and yelled, "What's all that noise? You sound like the Salvation Army!"

Dr. Brueggemann looked up at him and said, "Son, we *are* the salvation army!"

Yes! In procession through the ages, we keep coming, waving our palms in celebration of our faith story of a Man who was willing to live for us and die for us that we might have Life Abundant.

We do not, as a people of faith, have to be intimidated by those who would silence us. We have a story to tell, and it's a story about ending slavery, whether it's in Egypt or Scotland or St. Louis. We do not have to be silenced by the seduction of security or success. We do not have to be coerced and controlled by consumerism. Our story is not one of pride and prejudice, but one of peace.

One of my favorite biblical faith stories is that of Joseph. I've always wanted a multicolored robe, not so that my brothers could bow down to me, but so that when I wore my rainbow robe, everyone who saw me could *see* my faith story and *know* to whom I belong. Now, I don't have a rainbow robe, but I do think we as Christians need to wear our faith so that the world may see and know to whom we all belong.

The story of Jesus Christ is this:
The people of this earth waited for a Messiah . . . a
    Savior . . .
    and only God would send a little baby king.
The child grew and began to question things as they
        were,
    and the man moved through his days and through
        this world,
        questioning the system of kings and priests and
        marketplace.
He was called the New Creation
            the New Covenant
            the Son of God
who brought to all who listened
                who saw
                who understood
                            change and
                            new life.
But kings and corporations and churches of this world
    work very hard
    to keep things as they are out into forever AMEN.
And so they killed him, he who said, Love one another,
            he who said, Feed my sheep,
        for they didn't want to share their bread and their
        wine.
Now the story should have ended there
    except that the story has always been
        that our God is the God of the covenant.
The Good News is that
    in spite of our faithlessness
        God is faithful
    and Jesus Christ was resurrected,
        for God so loved the world
            that he gave his only begotten Son

that whoever believed
might have everlasting Life.
Listen, you who have ears to hear.
Listen, and sit down to bread and wine with strangers.
Feed his sheep. . . . Love one another,
and claim new life in his name.